CREATING STORAGE

By the Editors of Sunset Books

Sunset Books
President and Publisher: Susan J. Maruyama
Director, Finance & Business Affairs: Gary Loebner
Director, Sales & Marketing: Richard A. Smeby
Marketing & Creative Services Manager: Guy C. Joy
Production Director: Lory Day
Editorial Director: Bob Doyle

Sunset Publishing Corporation
Chairman: Jim Nelson
President/Chief Executive Officer: Robin Wolaner
Chief Financial Officer: James E. Mitchell
Publisher: Stephen J. Seabolt
Circulation Director: Robert I. Gursha
Vice President, Manufacturing: Lorinda R. Reichert
Editor, Sunset Magazine: William R. Marken

Creating Storage was produced with the assistance of
St. Remy Press
President: Pierre Léveillé
Managing Editor: Carolyn Jackson
Senior Editor: Heather Mills
Senior Art Director: Francine Lemieux

Book Consultants
Giles Miller-Mead
Don Vandervort

Special Contributors
Eric Beaulieu, Michel Blais, Marc Cassini, Robert Chartier,
François Daxhelet, Hélène Dion, Jean-Guy Doiron,
Lorraine Doré, Dominique Gagné, Michel Giguère,
Christine M. Jacobs, Solange Laberge, François Longpré,
Geneviève Monette, Jacques Perrault, Rebecca Smollett,
Michelle Turbide, Natalie Watanabe, Judy Yelon

COVER: Storage unit designed by Philip Harvey. Cover
design by Susan Bryant. Photo direction and styling by
JoAnn Masaoka Van Atta. Photography by Philip Harvey.

For more information on *Creating Storage* or any other
Sunset Book, call 1-800-634-3095. For special sales, bulk
orders, and premium sales information, call Sunset Custom
Publishing Services at (415) 324-5577.

Acknowledgments
Thanks to the following:
Akro-Mils, Akron, OH
APA-The Engineered Wood Association, Tacoma, WA
Daniel Ball, Ellicott City, MD
James Bartsch, Cornell University (Department of
 Agricultural and Biological Engineering), Ithaca, NY
Beaver Industries, St. Paul, MN
Canadian Red Cross Society, Verdun, Que.
Christensen's Urban Insect Solutions, Lexington, KY
Closetmaid, Ocala, FL
Crawford Products, West Hanover, MA
Edsal Manufacturing Co., Chicago, IL
Frem Corporation, Worcester, MA
Craig Goldwyn, World Wine Championships, Chicago, IL
Henssgen Hardware Corp., Glens Falls, NY
Home Ventilating Institute, Arlington Heights, IL
Ikea Canada, Burlington, Ont.
Infant and Toddler Safety Association, Kitchener, Ont.
Insulation Contractors Association, Alexandria, VA
Intermetro Industries Corp., Wilkes-Barre, PA
Iron-a-way, Morton, IL
Justrite Manufacturing Co., Des Plaines, IL
Abel Kader, Department of Pomology, University of
 California, Davis, CA
Knape and Vogt Manufacturing Co., Grand Rapids, MI
Lee/Rowan Co., Fenton, MO
National Association of Chiefs of Police, Miami, FL
National Association of Waterproofing Contractors,
 Indianapolis, IN
National Fire Protection Association, Quincy, MA
National Pest Control Association, Dunn Loring, VA
National Rifle Association, Fairfax, VA
Rubbermaid Inc., Wooster, OH
La Société Québecoise de Récupération et de Recyclage,
 Quebec, Que.
Peter Smollett, Toronto, Ont.
Spacemaker Ltd., Mississauga, Ont.
Marc St-Pierre, Montreal, Que.

Picture Credits
p. 20 courtesy Ikea Canada
p. 21 *(upper)* courtesy Intermetro Industries Corp.
p. 21 *(lower)* courtesy Lee/Rowan Co.
p. 22 *(left)* courtesy Knape and Vogt Manufacturing Co.
p. 22 *(upper right)* courtesy Lee/Rowan Co.
p. 22 *(lower right)* courtesy Justrite Manufacturing Co.
p. 23 *(upper)* courtesy Edsal Manufacturing Co.
p. 23 *(lower left)* courtesy Akro-Mils
p. 23 *(lower right)* courtesy Knape and Vogt Manufacturing Co.
p. 24 *(upper)* courtesy Frem Corporation
p. 24 *(lower left)* courtesy Frem Corporation
p. 24 *(lower right)* courtesy Ikea Canada
p. 25 *(upper)* courtesy Spacemaker Ltd.
p. 25 *(lower left)* courtesy Knape and Vogt Manufacturing Co.
p. 25 *(lower right)* courtesy Rubbermaid Inc.
p. 26 *(all)* courtesy Lee/Rowan Co.
p. 27 *(upper left)* courtesy Closetmaid
p. 27 *(lower left)* courtesy Closetmaid
p. 27 *(right)* courtesy Iron-a-way
p. 28 *(upper left)* courtesy Lee/Rowan Co.
p. 28 *(upper right)* courtesy Ikea Canada
p. 28 *(lower)* Tom Wyatt
p. 29 *(left)* courtesy Frem Corporation
p. 29 *(right)* courtesy Ikea Canada

CONTENTS

4 PLANNING FOR STORAGE
5 Getting Organized
6 Basements
9 Attics
12 Garages
16 Storage Hazards

19 STORAGE IDEAS
20 Commercial Storage Solutions
30 Books, Documents, and Photos
32 Food and Wine
38 Recycling
41 Firewood
43 Workshop
50 Laundry
52 Clothing
54 Outerwear and Sports Equipment
59 Furniture and Other Bulky Items
67 Gardening Tools and Supplies

71 TOOLS AND TECHNIQUES
72 Tools
73 Fasteners
74 Basic Joinery
78 Pegs and Hooks
81 Boxes, Bins, and Cases
83 Shelves
86 Doors
88 Drawers

89 IMPROVING STORAGE AREAS
90 Basements
92 Attics
94 Garages

96 INDEX

PLANNING FOR STORAGE

The first step to take in creating new storage space in your home is to examine each area of the house for hidden storage potential. Basements, attics, and garages make ideal areas for storing objects that you don't need access to every day—from garment bags of out-of-season clothes to boxes of documents that you're holding onto "just in case." If designed correctly, these areas can also provide accessible storage space for supplies, such as firewood or laundry products. In this chapter, we'll give you general tips on sorting through and organizing the jumble of objects that may currently be stashed in odd corners in your house. We'll show you how to take maximum advantage of the storage potential of your basement, attic, or garage by fitting storage units to the space available: between studs in your garage, under the eaves in your attic, or under stairs in your basement or garage. We'll also help you ward off storage hazards.

In the chapter starting on page 19, we'll suggest ideas for storing specific items, everything from bicycles to rugs. For basic techniques on building shelves, bins, and other storage units, turn to page 71. Finally, beginning on page 89, we'll demonstrate how to make your basement, attic, and garage better storage areas by improving lighting, heating, and access.

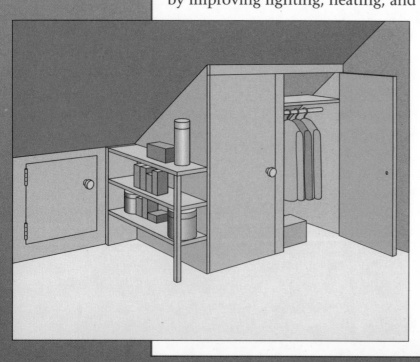

Sloping walls in an attic pose a challenge to designing storage units. The closet shown at left uses the space under the eaves efficiently, while the cupboard door provides access to the space behind the knee wall.

GETTING ORGANIZED

In many homes, the basement, attic, and garage are prime spots for storing inaccessible piles of possessions. Just building new storage units to stash all this stuff doesn't make it more accessible. Instead, a more organized approach to planning storage space is necessary. First, it's a good idea to sort through your possessions and decide what you really need to keep. Then, plan where in the house these objects can be most conveniently kept, and buy or build any new storage units that are needed. Finally, objects need to be organized in drawers and cupboards in a logical way. In the rest of this book, we'll show you how to create new storage units. But, on this page, we'll provide tips on making sure you make the best use of the new storage space you'll uncover.

CUTTING DOWN ON CLUTTER

This may be the most painful step, but there's really no point in creating new storage space for objects you can do without. It's a good idea to start with small areas—a closet or toolbox—that you can have the satisfaction of sorting through completely. Plan on selling or giving away what you can. Here are a few reasons to get rid of clutter:

• Clutter costs you time. It has to be cleaned and shuffled about, and it keeps you from getting at things you need.
• Clutter costs you money. Creating new storage space for things you feel you must store is costly.
• Clutter tends to multiply. If an area is already messy, it's tempting to shove in one more object.
• Clutter can be dangerous. Poorly stored objects can fall on a child; toxic substances can remain hidden in the mess rather than being safely stored.
• If an item is broken, it may be cheaper to replace when needed than to repair it.
• For all the odds and ends we keep "just in case," it's probably easier to replace the few we end up needing than to store them all indefinitely.

DESIGNING STORAGE AREAS

Storage usually falls into one of three categories: active, seasonal, and dead. Active storage includes things you need access to regularly, such as sewing supplies or food; keep it separate from other storage. Seasonal storage is typically out-of-season clothes and sports equipment. Dead storage includes things that are rarely needed, such as toys waiting for the next child or memorabilia that might be pulled out every 20 years. Basements and attached garages are usually the best choices for active storage, although a separate garage may be adequate for a workshop or gardening center. An attic, if you have one, is ideal for dead or seasonal storage. When planning what goes where, keep the following points in mind:

• For active storage, keep things where they are used. If you usually do your mending on the living room couch, for example, why not find a place for some sewing supplies near there?
• Make sure that storage areas in the garage and basement are well lit—particularly since some of these spots double as activity areas, such as for laundry or crafts.
• Include a catch-all bin for objects that are needed frequently during an activity.

BUILDING NEW STORAGE UNITS

Before building new units, make sure the existing space is used efficiently. Then, when designing new storage units, build them to suit not only the space available, but also the objects you plan to store there.

• Search out unused nooks and crannies, such as under stairs and between wall studs.
• Make a scale drawing of the area to plan the space. Self-adhesive notepaper is handy for scale cutouts of furniture that can then be moved around on the plan.
• For storing large objects, such as cardboard boxes, make sure the shelves are deep enough so that the objects don't topple off.
• Make sure shelves are sturdy enough for the load they'll have to bear.
• For smaller objects, make deep storage areas accessible with lazy Susans and pullout units.
• Divide up vertical spaces with stacking bins or baskets or wall-mounted shelves.
• In a dusty area, such as a workshop, or for storing books, documents, and other objects that need to be kept particularly clean, consider using closed cabinets and drawers.

USING THE NEW SPACE

Finally, you're ready to use your new storage space. The following considerations are important when installing each object in its new home:

• Keep those things you use the most at the front of drawers and shelves.
• Store only lightweight objects high overhead.
• Take into account the height of the members of your household when deciding what should go where.
• Make sure all dead storage is clearly labeled on a surface that will be visible once the boxes are piled up.

BASEMENTS

A basement, loosely defined, is the area between the base of a house's foundation and the floor joists that support the living space above. Four different basement schemes are shown below. In the case of a full basement, the concrete slab and foundation walls form an enclosed, defined room—but one usually left unimproved by the builders. A full basement has sufficient headroom for a livable space, usually 7½ feet.

In many newer homes, the foundation is made shallow to save money and labor, and perhaps to avoid problems with the underground water table. In such cases, only a minimal foundation wall extends above the footings, so basement space is greatly reduced. This kind of mini-basement, or crawl space, can still be very useful for storage. Split-level homes often have both a full basement and a crawl space.

Exceptions to the usual basement scheme are pier and slab foundations. Slab foundations are unusable for storage. Pier foundations afford some space, but they are open to the elements, insects, and animals—as well as theft. Storage in a pier foundation should be in enclosed, lockable units.

PROTECTING AGAINST MOISTURE AND RODENTS

Many homes have the kind of unfinished basement shown opposite, with exposed ducts, floor joists, and masonry walls. Before installing storage units in such a space, consider ways of improving it by controlling temperature and moisture, and putting in more attractive floors and walls. See page 89 for suggestions.

In most unfinished basements, moisture poses a threat to stored belongings. Waterproofing or dehumidifying may not be worth the expense if the moisture problem is minor and the items to be stored are hardy. For damp,

unimproved basements, choose metal storage units instead of wood. Metal won't swell and warp like wood, although it may rust. Don't pile up containers—let air circulate around them. And don't install closets and cabinets on the floor or against an uninsulated masonry wall; instead, moistureproof the cabinets, as shown opposite. If your basement is subject to occasional flooding or standing water, consider placing loose items on a raised platform.

A basement with a dirt floor is a rat's delight. A foundation wall and concrete slab in good condition help keep vermin at bay. Most rodents enter through rotted sheathing just above the foundation wall, dilapidated vent screens, and vent pipes; check these regularly. Metal containers, such as metal garbage cans, taped shut, will keep rodents away from stored items. You can also try lining plywood boxes with sheet metal.

USING THE SPACE

The layout of your basement may offer ready-to-use storage space: Look overhead, underneath the stairs, and around and between heating ducts. An unfinished basement is roofed with the floor joists and subfloor materials of the rooms above, as shown opposite. The spaces between exposed joists and the clearance between your head and the joists are excellent for storing small goods. Pick spots that are free of ducts, plumbing, and wiring. Nail wood strips across several joists to create overhead shelves; two boards mounted edge to edge make a rack. Shelves suspended with rope or chain, or "ladder shelves" *(page 8)*, are easy to make. A frequently overlooked space is the wedge-shaped area under a staircase; this spot provides a place to build shelves, rollout bins, cupboards, or a closet.

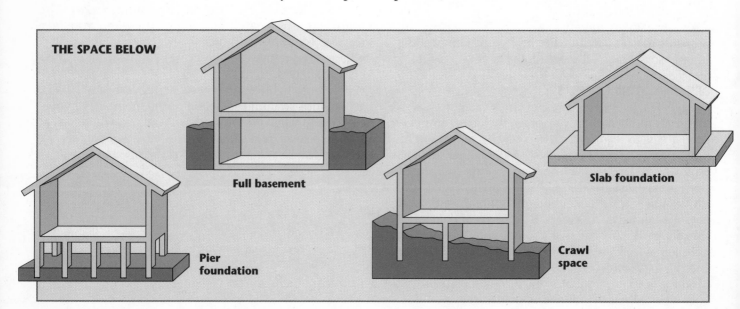

THE SPACE BELOW

Full basement

Pier foundation

Crawl space

Slab foundation

AN UNFINISHED BASEMENT

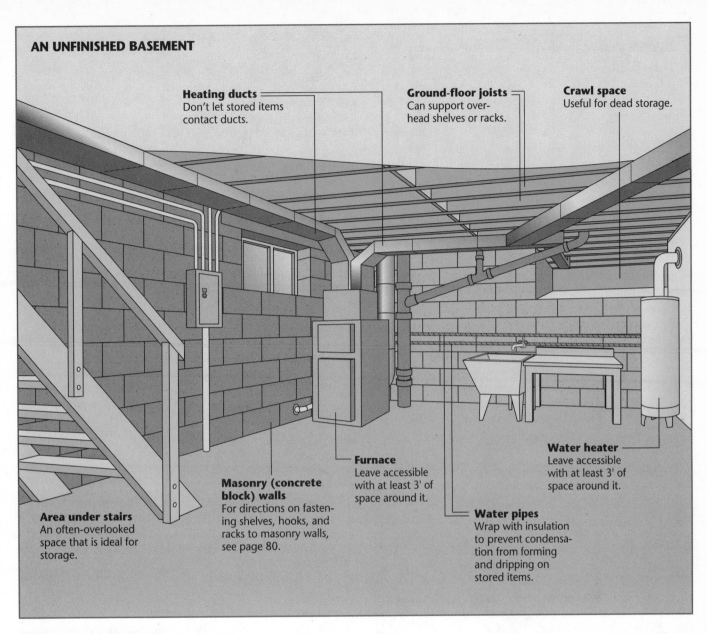

Heating ducts
Don't let stored items contact ducts.

Ground-floor joists
Can support overhead shelves or racks.

Crawl space
Useful for dead storage.

Furnace
Leave accessible with at least 3' of space around it.

Water heater
Leave accessible with at least 3' of space around it.

Water pipes
Wrap with insulation to prevent condensation from forming and dripping on stored items.

Masonry (concrete block) walls
For directions on fastening shelves, hooks, and racks to masonry walls, see page 80.

Area under stairs
An often-overlooked space that is ideal for storage.

ASK A PRO

HOW CAN I MOISTUREPROOF A CABINET?

To protect a storage cabinet from basement dampness, raise it 3 to 4 inches off the floor on a treated-wood base and place it against furring strips fastened to the wall. Spread heavy polyethylene sheeting under and behind the cabinet to provide added protection; fasten it to the upper strip to keep it in place.

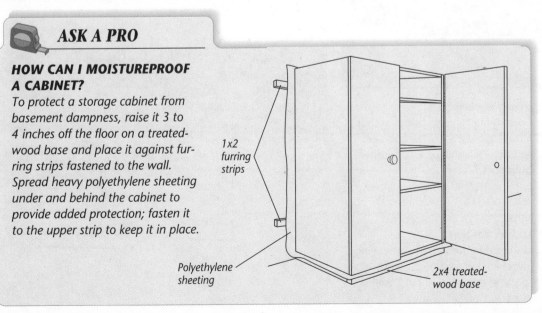

1x2 furring strips

Polyethylene sheeting

2x4 treated-wood base

Basement storage ideas

Closet and cubbyhole

An L-shaped stairway provides for two separate storage areas under the stairs; one is used as a clothes closet, while the other is a shelved cubbyhole.

Pullouts

Shelving units on casters allow easy access to the full depth of the storage area under the stairs.

Utility shelves

Custom-built shelves take maximum advantage of under-stairs storage; some stairways allow access from both sides.

Ladder shelves

U-shaped frames fastened to ceiling joists with lag screws utilize overhead space; in this setup, a 1x12 shelf sits in a cradle of 2x4s.

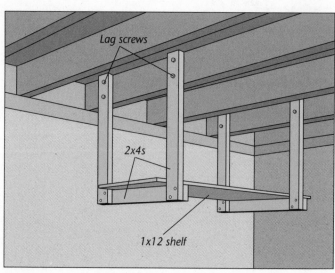

Lag screws

2x4s

1x12 shelf

ATTICS

An attic's shape—and its capacity for storage—depend on how steeply the roof is pitched and on the house's dimensions. Roof pitch determines the attic's height, while the size of the house determines its floor space. Steep roofs make the best attics; flat roofs offer none at all. For a living space, a room should normally have a 7½-foot ceiling over at least one-half of the available floor space. For storage, though, you can use whatever space is accessible. Even a minimal crawl space, common in newer homes, has usable storage space.

An unfinished attic is subject to extreme swings in temperature, making it unsuitable for storing delicate items such as books. You may want to consider insulating the attic to control the temperature. You can also put in a plywood floor or improve access with a fold-down stairway if there isn't already one in place. These improvements are discussed beginning on page 92.

It's important to lay out your attic in an orderly way so that you can easily find everything. Arrange related objects in one place and store those you use often where they're easy to reach. Label covered items and boxes with permanent ink on white tape for identification. Small, fragile keepsakes requiring extra protection from moisture, dust, and insects should be carefully packed in sturdy boxes and sealed; cover furniture with mattress pads and wrap with polyethylene. It can be helpful to keep an inventory of everything in the attic.

USING THE SPACE

An attic's configuration is usually a challenge for orderly storage. How do you deal with sloping walls, corners you have to crawl into, triangular gable walls, and the high but narrow ridge line overhead? The trick is to fit your storage to the shape of the attic.

Many newer homes are built with relatively flat roofs that leave only a minimal attic or a crawl space. Usually even a crawl space has usable storage space in the middle and at the gable ends. You can at least lay down plywood around the access hatch. If you can reach the gables easily, build storage cupboards and a floor or catwalk

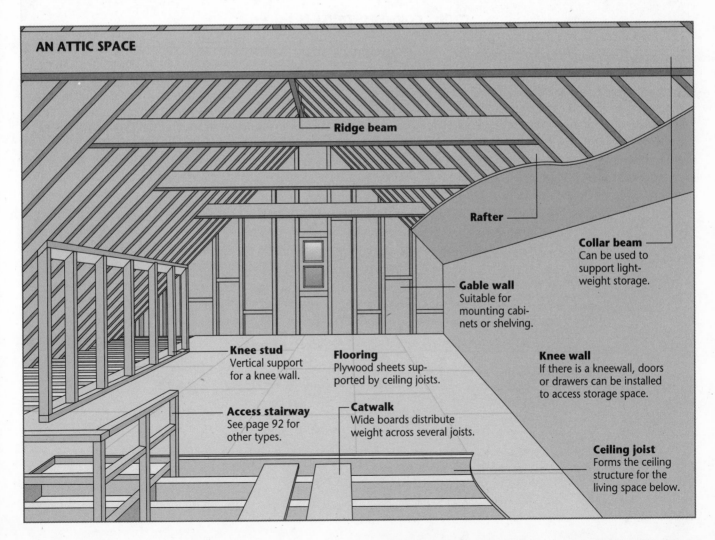

AN ATTIC SPACE

Ridge beam

Rafter

Collar beam
Can be used to support light-weight storage.

Gable wall
Suitable for mounting cabinets or shelving.

Knee stud
Vertical support for a knee wall.

Flooring
Plywood sheets supported by ceiling joists.

Knee wall
If there is a kneewall, doors or drawers can be installed to access storage space.

Access stairway
See page 92 for other types.

Catwalk
Wide boards distribute weight across several joists.

Ceiling joist
Forms the ceiling structure for the living space below.

leading from the hatch. Some ideas for using attics and crawl spaces efficiently for storage follow; others are illustrated on page 11.

Sloping walls: You can either shape storage units to conform to the sloping space under the rafters or build vertical units across this space. Cabinet doors and recessed drawers are efficient ways to access space behind knee walls. The storage area behind the knee wall should not be deeper than your reach, unless the opening is large enough for a walk-in.

Simpler solutions? Shelves hung with rope or chain, or items hanging from a closet rod, square off attic space. Or you can build shelves under adjacent rafters.

Gable walls: Install custom-made shelves to fit along the gable wall, or place shelves or cabinets along the base of the wall.

Articles that would be damaged by extremes of heat or cold (artwork, for example) shouldn't be stored against a gable wall unless the wall is insulated. This is particularly true if the gable wall is on the north side of the house or if it's exposed to direct sun for long periods. Also, be sure not to block any vents in the wall.

Ridge line: Cut off the triangular peak with rope-hung or chain-hung shelves (accessible from the sides), or hang items from long nails, hooks, or pegs fixed high on the rafters. A closet rod or a long 1x2 fastened to opposing rafters will support garment bags full of seasonal clothes, as shown on page 53. If there's a ridge vent, don't block it.

Collar beams: You can form a loft in your attic by placing boards or plywood between existing collar beams or between beams you've added yourself. Such a platform should be used for lightweight storage only.

PLAY IT SAFE

STEPPING CAREFULLY IN YOUR ATTIC
Never walk or place storage in the areas between joists in an attic—that's your downstairs ceiling, which is not intended to support weight. For information on putting in an attic floor or catwalk, see page 93.

TIGHT CORNERS: TRUSS FRAMING

Truss framing makes it difficult to use an attic for storage; the trusses integrate rafters, collar beams, and sometimes ceiling joists into single framing members, usually spaced 24 inches apart. You cannot remove or cut into trusses, so storage units must be built around or between them.

Although accessing these areas can be challenging, laying plywood shelves as shown below is one way of making the most of the space. If there is insulation in the way, don't compress it. Instead, attach cleats to the framing above the insulation to support the plywood shelves.

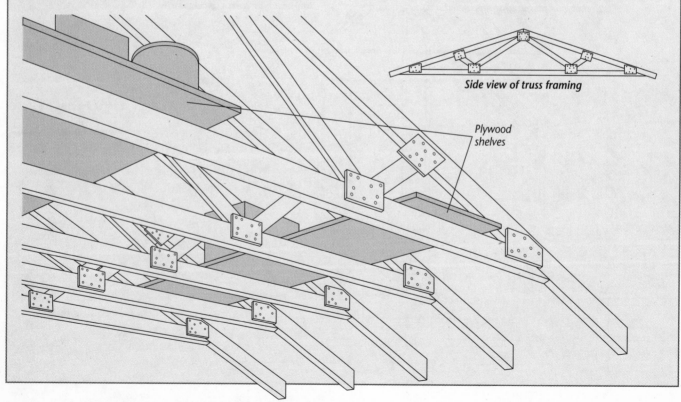

Side view of truss framing

Plywood shelves

Attic storage ideas

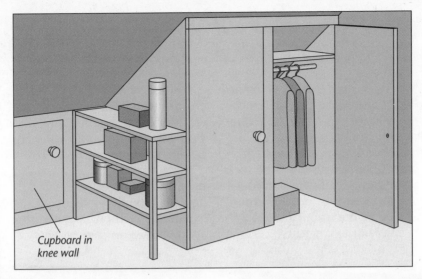

Cupboard in knee wall

Custom closet and cupboard

In this finished attic, a closet is built to fit against the sloping wall under the rafters. A low cupboard door gives access to the space behind the knee wall.

Rafters

Plywood shelves

Vertical support

Shelves between rafters

The back corners of these shelves sit on cleats fastened to the rafters; the front edges are fixed to vertical supports. The shelves are notched to fit around rafters between their ends.

Gable wall

Gable shelves

These shelving units are built to fit the space around a gable window and between sloping walls. The top ends of the uprights are beveled to butt against the sloping walls.

Lag screws

Ridge beam

Chain

2x12 shelves

Rafters

Chain-hung shelves

These shelves are suspended from large screws driven into the rafters. These units make use of space along the ridge beam that is usually wasted.

GARAGES

Most garages have room for storage around or above vehicles. Awkward spots and places that are inaccessible when the car is inside (such as rafter space) are best for seasonal or long-term storage.

If your garage also houses work areas, the key to an efficient layout is grouping items that go together, such as gardening supplies. Some garage work areas to consider are illustrated below. In a garage attached to the house, you may want to set up a mudroom and closet for boots, rain gear, and other outdoor clothes.

Position work areas to maximize convenience and ensure safe working conditions. A garden maintenance area, for example, should be handy to the garden or yard. The items you use most often should, of course, be close at hand.

If you're using your garage as a working area, you may want to improve the ventilation, heating, and lighting. You may even want to add an extension to expand your storage possibilities. These improvements are discussed on page 94.

A WELL-ORGANIZED GARAGE

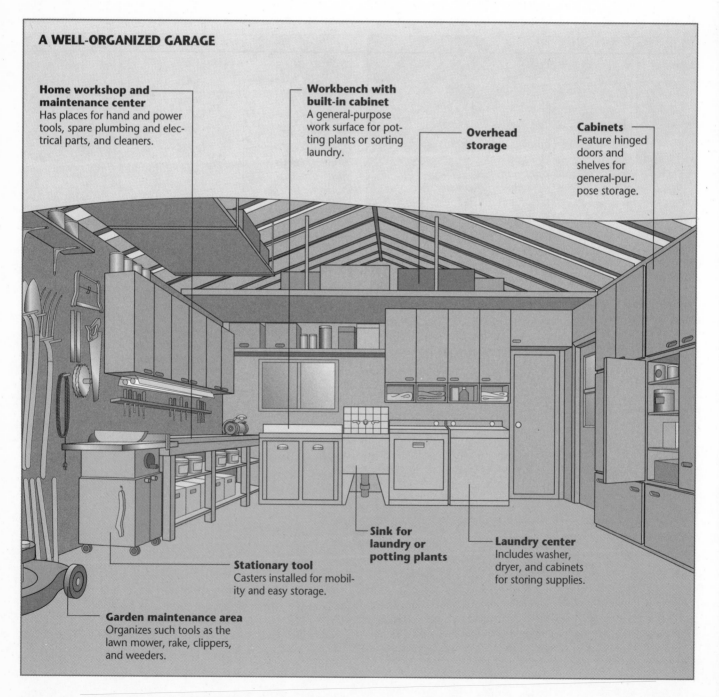

Home workshop and maintenance center
Has places for hand and power tools, spare plumbing and electrical parts, and cleaners.

Workbench with built-in cabinet
A general-purpose work surface for potting plants or sorting laundry.

Overhead storage

Cabinets
Feature hinged doors and shelves for general-purpose storage.

Stationary tool
Casters installed for mobility and easy storage.

Sink for laundry or potting plants

Laundry center
Includes washer, dryer, and cabinets for storing supplies.

Garden maintenance area
Organizes such tools as the lawn mower, rake, clippers, and weeders.

THE SPACE ABOVE

In addition to space around your vehicle, each type of garage roof shown below has storage potential. Shed, hip, and gable roofs provide for overhead storage. Flat roofs only have the room between joists for storage.

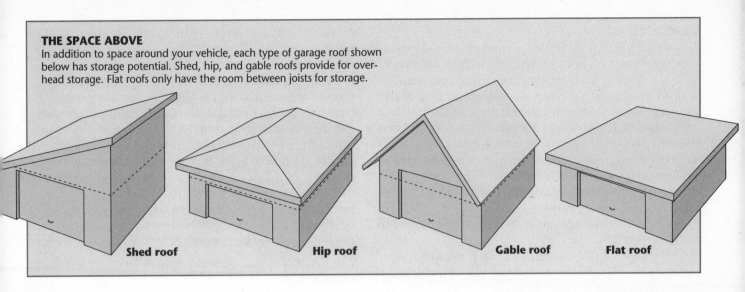

Shed roof **Hip roof** **Gable roof** **Flat roof**

CALCULATING CLEARANCE

Clearance is the space needed around a car when it is parked in a garage or carport; it affects how much room you'll have to work with when planning where to put storage units, appliances, and worktables.

See the drawing at right for minimum clearance recommendations around typical vehicles; the exact distance necessary for opening doors will depend on your model. To calculate how much storage space you have to work with, park your vehicle or vehicles in the garage. (Make sure to leave sufficient space between vehicles if you have more than one.) Then measure the distance from each vehicle to the walls and other obstructions. Subtract the recommended clearance figures and you have the bottom line—the real storage potential. If you're planning overhead storage, make sure to leave adequate clearance above both your head and the car; don't forget to allow for roof racks. In general, before installing built-in storage units, consider whether you are likely to purchase a larger vehicle in the future.

If you're planning to install storage units around the contour of your car's hood and roof, it may be a challenge to park safely. Try attaching a tennis ball to a cord with a fishhook or eye screw, and hanging the ball so that it will nudge your windshield when the car is properly parked. Alternatively, you can fasten a length of 2x4 to the garage floor to "curb" the front wheels when the car is in place.

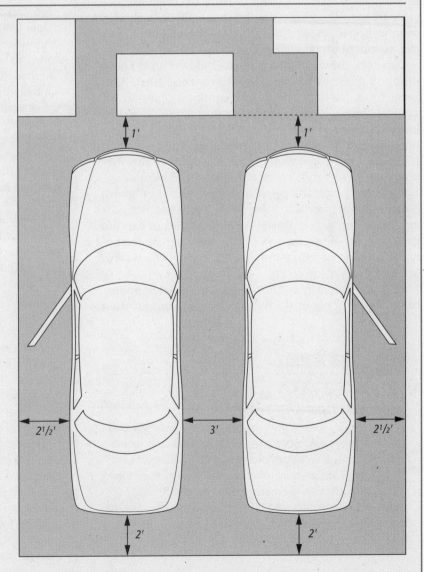

USING THE SPACE

To save floor space, raise storage units above the ground whenever possible. You can hang them high on a wall or suspend them from the joists or rafters, fitting units around the contours of your car's hood and roof. Make sure to allow for adequate clearance *(page 13)*.

In carports, the best spot for storage units is between the roof support posts. Attach units to the floor slab, suspend them from overhead beams, or add intermediate vertical framing to hold them up. In an open carport, units with doors that slide or that open to the outside leave more clearance inside.

The following is a brief guide to storage units suited to the garage or carport:

Shelves: Build freestanding frames for shelves, or hang shelf units with backs from the wall. Wood-framed garage walls provide for shallow shelves between studs. Some common types of hardware used to install shelves —adjustable tracks and brackets, L-braces, individual brackets, or continuous brackets—are shown on page 83. If your garage walls are made of brick or concrete block, place freestanding shelves against the wall, hang shelves from ceiling joists, or attach them to the wall using special masonry fasteners *(page 80)*.

Cabinets, drawers, and closets: Enclosed units keep dust and moisture out, and help to organize small items. Large tools, lawn mowers, and cleaning supplies fit into vertical closets. Recycled cabinets from a remodeled kitchen are perfect for the garage. Securely locked, enclosed units keep children safe from garden poisons and sharp tools, and guard against theft. Sliding doors or tilt-out bins make large units more accessible in tight places.

Racks and pegs: The perforated hardboard (Peg-Board) hanger system *(page 80)* is very versatile for hanging storage. Large fasteners or dowels set into wall studs can hold garden chairs—even ladders. Commercially manufactured racks, whether of heavy-duty metal or vinyl-coated wire, are useful but more costly.

Rollouts: One way to fit storage units, workbenches, or stationary tools into a tight garage is to mount them on heavy-duty casters. Store them close to the wall, then roll them out onto the main floor to use them when the car is out.

Overhead storage units: Most garages allow for overhead storage, as shown on page 13. You may want to facilitate storage over the joists by building a loft *(page 94)*. To install overhead shelving quickly, fasten boards across the top edges of joists, using screws or nails at least twice as long as the thickness of the boards. A nylon or canvas hammock draped above head level can be used to store lightweight items such as seasonal sports equipment or bagged winter blankets. Even in flat-roofed garages, overhead joists form cubbyholes that are great for small storage, especially for seasonal or infrequently used items.

STORAGE SHEDS

A shed keeps garden and yard gear near where you need it, freeing up room in the garage or basement. Before building a shed, check with the building department on whether you need a building permit, and whether there are limitations on the location of the shed. Restrictive covenants in your deed may also limit whether you can build a shed and where it can be located.

Prefab metal sheds are easy to assemble, but they tend to rust and it's difficult to attach storage units to their thin walls. So before purchasing a kit, find out whether the manufacturer produces a line of accessories designed for the shed.

If you're more ambitious, you can build a wood shed to meet your exact storage needs. However, keep in mind that a wood shed is flammable. For plans, you can contact wood associations such as APA—The Engineered Wood Association.

If allowed by code, a shed should be on some kind of foundation to secure it from wind and frost heave, and to prevent wood floors from rotting. Metal sheds often come without floors; a concrete slab is an ideal foundation for these. Some prefab sheds come with special ground anchors or floor supports. Concrete piers and wood beams make a simple foundation for a wood frame shed. If your shed floor is above ground level, or if the door has a high sill, you'll probably want to build some kind of ramp for wheeling in heavy equipment.

Floor space in a shed is valuable and you'll want to use it for access and heavy equipment. You can fasten cabinets, shelves, tool racks, and workbenches to the framing members in a wood shed. For a metal shed, use the manufacturer's storage accessories or consider building a wood frame inside the metal walls. If you have a hinged door that swings out, install narrow shelves on the back of the door.

 ASK A PRO

HOW DO I PROTECT CARPORT STORAGE FROM WEATHER AND THEFT?

Build enclosed cabinets from exterior-grade 3/4-inch plywood and finish them with exterior enamel or polyurethane; set the cabinets on bases made of pressure-treated lumber to raise them several inches above the floor. For maximum security, install sturdy locks and hasps on doors (page 18)*, and use inside-mounted hinges with nonremovable pins. Or, consider bolting a locked chest to joists or ledger strips* (opposite).

Garage and carport storage ideas

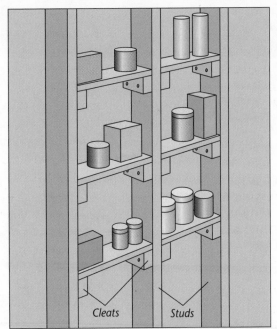

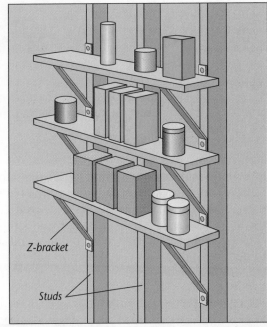

Z-bracket

Studs

Cleats   Studs

Shelving

Wall studs are usually spaced 16 or 24 inches apart, on center. Small, shallow shelves can rest on cleats fastened between the studs *(above, left)* or on Z-brackets attached to the front edges of the studs *(above, right)*.

Carport cabinets

The cabinets and workbench shown at right fit between the posts in a carport, with an additional support post. If your carport isn't enclosed, make sure the units are weatherproof.

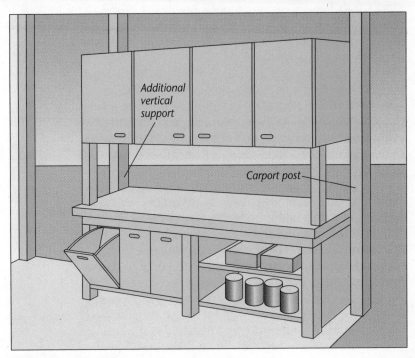

Additional vertical support

Carport post

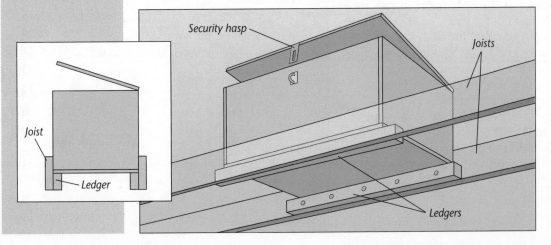

Security hasp

Joists

Joist

Ledger

Ledgers

Overhead box

The locking plywood box at left is ideal for securing valuables in a carport. It is built to fit between overhead joists and rest on ledgers bolted to the joists.

STORAGE HAZARDS

Piles of sawdust, a rickety ladder propped up in a corner, carelessly placed tools—these hazards all deserve attention. If you're setting your storage in order, make room for safety, too.

Basements, attics, and garages are very susceptible to accidents and fire. To prevent storage disasters, your first jobs are to sort, organize, and clean. Discard old paint cans, broken toys, and other items you're never going to need. Make sure your storage areas are well lit and that the floor is clear of any objects that someone could trip over. Following are some specific pointers and suggestions to help you with your task. For more safety guidelines, contact fire, health, and other appropriate officials.

TOOLS AND TOXIC SUBSTANCES

Your workshop or garden shed makes a perfect secret place for little ones playing hide-and-seek. Children—yours or a neighbor's—can easily get into toxic garden or workshop supplies, or play with sharp tools if these items aren't properly stored.

Place dangerous tools and poisons well out of the reach of children. Hang sharp tools, blades, and bits high on walls with strong hooks; make sure they won't fall. Do not store poisons anywhere accessible, such as under utility sinks or on the ground between wall studs; never store them near bulk food supplies. Remember, pets should be protected from these dangers, too.

Tools and toxic substances can both be stored in drawers and cabinets that have plastic safety latches *(right, top)*. A variety of these childproof latches is available—baby, toy, and department stores sometimes have a larger selection than hardware stores—but most work the same way. A hooked latch attaches to the inside of the door or drawer front and fastens to the inside of the cabinet frame. When the door or drawer is closed, the hook makes it impossible to open the door or drawer without unhooking the latch from the frame—something a young child will be unable to do. Make sure any latch you buy is made of sturdy plastic that won't break or lose its ability to spring back. Also, keep in mind that the easier it is for you to open, the more likely it will be used. Make sure that the latch doesn't let go when the door is yanked back and forth repeatedly. Check the device regularly to make sure the latch hasn't worked loose or become misaligned. On units you use less frequently, consider installing metal locks.

To keep children from opening doors to storage areas that are off-limits, install doorknob covers *(right, middle)*. Cabinet locks *(right, bottom)* will prevent access to cupboards, cabinets, or closets with twin doors.

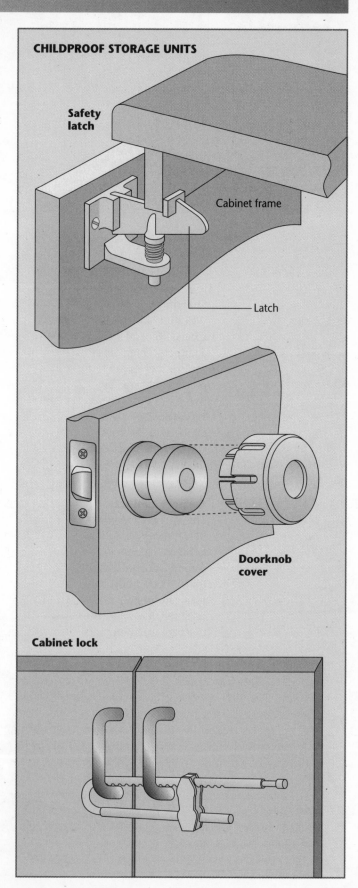

CHILDPROOF STORAGE UNITS

Safety latch

Cabinet frame

Latch

Doorknob cover

Cabinet lock

POWER TOOLS AND WIRING

When planning the electrical needs for a work area, be sure to provide enough electrical circuits; check with an electrician. You may need to install additional circuits in your basement or garage workshop for new tools, or in your attic for lighting. Power tools and lighting should be on separate circuits; a tool circuit should be at least 20 amps to prevent overload.

Power tools present a host of dangers. Any new outlets you install should be the grounded (three-prong) type. Also, don't use power tools in damp conditions. To guard against shock, purchase double-insulated power tools and install ground-fault circuit interrupter (GFCI) outlets; these outlets are designed to protect you by tripping instantly when they detect a leak in current. A master switch controlled by a key will prevent children from turning on tools.

Plugging too many tools or appliances into an extension cord is hazardous because the excessive current draw will generate heat, which can cause the cord's insulation to ignite. Generally, do not rely heavily on extension cords. Never string extension cords under rugs or tie them to nails; this can puncture them and result in a fire. Avoid using extra-long cords whose gauge is insufficient for the tool being used; again, the insulation could overheat and ignite. Periodically inspect extension cords for cracks, fraying, and broken plugs.

FLAMMABLE SUBSTANCES

In the workshop, make it a habit to frequently discard wood scraps and vacuum up sawdust, especially behind panels, boxes, and equipment where highly flammable sawdust collects.

Storing flammable liquids is a risky practice. Gasoline for lawn mowers and other equipment should be stored in a can that is specially designed for gasoline, with a spring closure valve, vapor vent, and pour spout; these are available at your hardware store. The can will be red metal or molded plastic. Blue cans for kerosene are also available. Cans of gasoline or kerosene should be stored outside the home in a detached shed or garage.

Never store flammable liquids in makeshift plastic or glass containers. Paint, wood finishes, solvent, rubber cement, and other flammable substances should be stored in their original containers, or in metal cans with tight-fitting lids and clearly marked labels. Store these liquids in a well-ventilated area far away from heat sources and in a spot where they can't be knocked over. For extra security, you can place them in a special fireproof metal cabinet such as the one shown on page 22. Never use flammable liquids near any heat sources, such as a pilot light; never smoke when a flammable liquid is being used.

Rags that have soaked up flammable substances should be kept immersed in water in metal containers

---

EARTHQUAKE-SECURE STORAGE

If you live in an earthquake region, be sure your storage can withstand a jolt without collapsing or spilling your stored treasures. The goal is to protect your possessions and protect your family *from* your possessions; in an earthquake, most people are hurt by falling objects. You won't be able to completely quake-proof your possessions, but by identifying and minimizing the risks, you can reduce the probability of damage and injury. Here are a few steps you should take:

• Begin by walking through your home and looking for potential hazards. Mentally shake every room to see what could fall.

• Secure anything that is top-heavy. Fasten freestanding bookcases and other storage shelving and cabinets to the wall with L-braces or metal plumber's tape screwed into wall studs. Tie off everything that is unstable or tall; use rope or wire and eye screws, bolts, or straps. Don't rely on nails for anchoring objects to walls; depend only on threaded fasteners, such as screws, driven into secure wall framing.

• Place heavy items low, breakables in secured spaces, and caustic chemicals in secure cabinets at floor level.

• Prevent objects on shelves from sliding or "walking" during earthquake shaking. Hold-fast putties, hook-and-

loop tape (Velcro), adhesive tapes, and other adhesives will keep items from moving. Restrain all items of electronic equipment by either fastening them directly or tethering them to secured shelves. Place secure barriers—such as a curtain rod or a raised molding—across the fronts of shelves to keep items from falling off.

• Be sure cabinets latch securely. Don't count on magnetic catches; they often shake free. You can retrofit cabinets with heavy spring-loaded hasp or touch latches, or replace the pulls with latches or catches that lock to the cabinet frame. In garage and other areas where storage doesn't have to be pretty, you can use tight-fitting eye hooks. For more visible cabinets, childproof latches (*opposite*) are inexpensive, invisible from outside the cabinet, and easy to use.

• At the very least, install secure catches on the cabinets that hold your precious breakables. To minimize damage, also pay attention to how items are stored within cabinets. You can put cushioning layers of foam or paper between seldom-used heirloom plates and install nonskid shelf padding, available at marine and RV-supply stores.

• Be sure ceiling-mounted storage is secured to joists or beams with threaded fasteners. Check the security of any item that hangs from the ceiling.

with tight-fitting lids away from heat sources. Better yet, throw them away, but first hang them up to dry outside before putting them in the garbage.

Store ashes in a metal container; don't place ashes in cardboard boxes or in a place where a breeze can stir up embers. Be sure to clean up any oil drippings.

HEATING EQUIPMENT

Make sure that combustibles are not positioned near heating equipment such as a furnace, water heater, or chimney. Leave 3 feet of space on all sides of the heating equipment.

To prevent fire in a storage area, it's wise to have a professional inspect and clean your heating equipment at least once every year. If you use your storage space as a work area, you may want to use a portable heater. If so, do not leave it unattended or place it where it can be tipped over.

LADDERS AND STAIRCASES

Make sure ladders and staircases are adequate for the loads they will have to bear, and that they are in good condition. Never block a ladder or staircase with boxes or overflow storage.

Position a ladder so that its base is offset from the perpendicular by one-quarter of its length; the foot of a 20-foot ladder, for example, should be 5 feet away from the point directly beneath the top of the ladder. Fold-down ladders usually aren't intended for heavy use.

Handrails on staircases should be solidly secured, and the steps clear and well lighted with light switches at the top and bottom. A minimum of $6^1/2$ feet of headroom all the way up is often required by code.

LIFESAVING DEVICES

Smoke and heat detectors, automatic sprinklers, fire extinguishers, and modifications to attic fans can make your storage areas much safer; in some areas, like the basement, you may want to install a flood alarm. Other safety measures that may be required by code include the use of solid-core doors leading from a carport or garage into living space to slow the spread of fire and covering combustible insulation with fire-retardant material, such as gypsum wallboard.

Smoke and heat detectors: These devices set off an alarm to alert people to danger, giving them time to escape. Smoke detectors alone, when properly placed, installed, and maintained, offer the minimum level of safety recommended by the National Fire Protection Association. Heat detectors may be located in areas unsuitable for smoke detectors, such as kitchens, bathrooms, garages, and attics, where normal temperatures may be too high or low for smoke detectors to work properly. Fixed-temperature heat detectors activate when the surrounding air reaches a certain temperature, usually 135°F.

Automatic sprinkler systems: Typically seen in public buildings, residential systems are also available. They are triggered by heat from a fire and are designed to slow the spread of fire, providing time to escape. Sprinklers also protect your possessions. Designed to discharge a minimum amount of water, considerably less than fire department hose lines, they will only go off in the room where the fire is located.

Fire extinguishers: Fire emergencies require quick action. Not all fire extinguishers are appropriate for all types of fire. Choose an ABC-rated dry-chemical fire extinguisher, which is effective against all fires that could occur in the home: burning wood or other combustibles, oil or grease fires, and electrical fires. Install extinguishers in or near your basement, attic, and garage near an escape route. Make sure that the extinguisher carries the label of a testing laboratory such as Underwriters Laboratory (UL) and is serviced yearly.

The only time you should try to put out a fire by yourself is if it is small and contained, and you have your back to a safe escape route. And, of course, you must know how to use an extinguisher. If the fire does not die down immediately, make your escape.

Modified attic fans: An attic fan can be a lethal instrument if a fire starts in your house while the fan is in operation. Air currents speed combustion and can turn a small fire into a raging one in a few seconds. To eliminate this hazard, equip fan power circuits with an automatic cutoff switch activated by a fire detection system.

VALUABLES

Depending on the contents and location of your storage cabinets or closets, you may want to make them secure. To foil burglars, use a security hasp and a heavy-duty padlock with a solid case and a steel shackle attached to an integral bolt *(below)*. When closed, the hasp should cover the screws that attach it to the unit. Standard hinged doors, with hinges mounted to the inside edges of the frame and door, and fitted with nonremovable hinge pins, are the most secure.

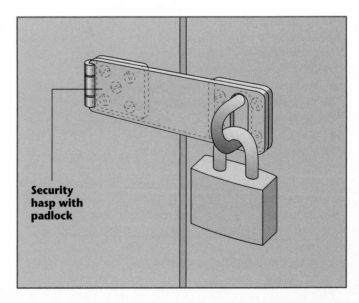

Security hasp with padlock

STORAGE IDEAS

Once you've examined your basement, attic, and garage for potential storage space, it's time to decide where to cache each item. Do you know where you'll stack the firewood to stoke the new wood stove you've been thinking about? How will you put to use the knowledge gained at that great wine class if you don't have a proper place to store wine? In addition to these evolving storage needs, you probably need dead storage for your multiplying financial records, mystery novels, and family photos.

Well-designed storage fits not only the space available, but the item being stored. Small items are best contained in drawers or bins. Large items can be stored on deep, open shelves or in cupboards built to fit. Long-handled tools can be hung from racks or propped against the wall. Don't forget to consider storing items overhead or high on walls to leave floor space for other activities.

This chapter begins with a section of color photos featuring a selection of commercial storage products that are available. The rest of the chapter gives item-by-item ideas for storage units you can build yourself. Most of the units shown are made up of simple elements: cases, shelves, and bins. The chapter beginning on page 71 will show you how to build each of these basic elements. Then once you've mastered these techniques, you'll be able to adapt the ideas in this chapter to your situation.

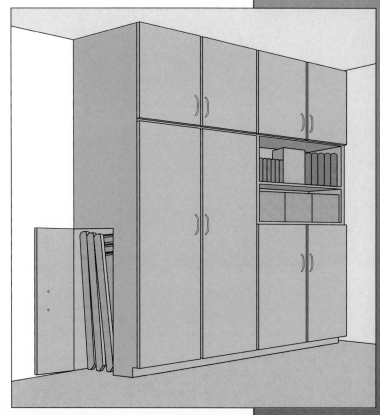

Stored behind a side door in a large cabinet, the game tables shown at right stand upright and can be accessed individually. Without the side door, everything in front of the tables would have to be pulled out to get at them.

COMMERCIAL STORAGE SOLUTIONS

The pages that follow show some of the wide variety of commercial storage products available on the market. A look through your local hardware store or home center will turn up many additional possibilities. These products are often the simplest solution to your storage needs—and sometimes the cheapest as well. Many storage systems include elements that can be mixed and matched to meet your specific situation. Shelves, racks, and stacking crates and bins can be combined to accommodate items of all sizes and shapes.

When purchasing a storage product, make sure the materials are strong enough for the weight you want them to support. Also, check the manufacturer's directions for ease of installation.

Storage units are available in a wide variety of materials: wood, metal, and plastic-coated wire. Wood and metal are generally stronger than wire. When buying wood shelf units, such as those shown above, choose boards that are free of structural defects like splits, loose knots, and warping. Shelves assembled with bolts are generally more durable than those using screws.

Many modular-style storage systems can be assembled to fit into irregular spaces. The metal shelves shown at right were put together so as to fit in the space under a stairway. Other useful features include brackets for looping cable, hanging baskets for small items, and suspended shelves for shorter items like the squat toolbox shown.

Storage units available in kits are a quick solution to many storage situations. Components can often be mixed and matched. In the garage shown at left, shelves holding craft projects are paired with a vertical cabinet containing sports equipment. Recycled kitchen cabinets are another storage option for the garage or basement.

Wire shelving is available with epoxy or vinyl coating, or with a painted-on coating that is much less durable. The shelves can sometimes be cut to length by the retailer to fit your space.

The shelves shown are supported by metal brackets fastened to the wall. If you're planning to store small items on wire shelves, make sure the wires are sufficiently close together to keep the objects from tipping over or falling through.

Track-and-bracket shelving makes it possible to adjust the height of shelves as storage needs change. Particleboard shelves, like those shown above, are relatively inexpensive. For maximum holding power, drive the screws securing the tracks into wall studs, which are typically spaced at 16-inch intervals. For instructions on installing track-and-bracket shelving, see page 84.

Keep flammable liquids like finishes and paint thinners in their original metal containers. Consider storing the containers in a double-lined fireproof cabinet like the one shown at right. For more information on storing hazardous materials, turn to page 16.

For a small workshop,
a cabinet like the one shown above may be
all you need. It can be hung on the wall or
set on a bench. Tools are hung from the per-
forated-steel back panel, while the doors feature shelves that accommodate screwdrivers
and small containers. In selecting such a cabinet, check that the doors can be locked to
keep children away from the contents.

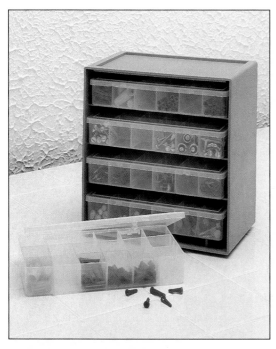

Hardware or sewing supplies are inaccessible
when piled up in little bags and boxes; drawers keep them organized. Translucent plastic
drawers like those shown above let you see
what's inside. The units are often designed
to be hung from the wall or stacked.

There is hidden storage space under almost any surface. The handy stool shown above holds small tools
as well as a few frequently used supplies. Similar
plastic or metal tool racks can be hung from a wall.

Stacking crates and bins are ideal for storing small objects and dividing up the space between large shelves. Plastic crates like those shown above are easy to clean.

Wood cabinets with drawers (right) offer an attractive way to store small objects and keep them out of sight. Smaller units can be placed on shelves.

Files stored in odd-shaped cardboard boxes are hard to get at when you need them. A crate like the one shown below, specifically designed for files, keeps them accessible. Choose one with a lid to keep dust out. Crates designed to be stacked are handy for dead storage.

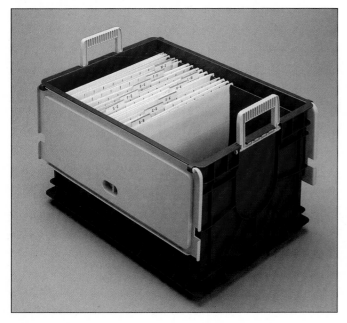

Prefabricated metal sheds of the type shown at left are an easy alternative to building your own. To protect the shed from wind and frost-heave, you would have to set it on a solid base made of cast concrete or concrete patio squares. Make sure the base is level and designed to drain water properly.

A metal tool rack (left) can be handy for holding a variety of tools. For best support, fasten racks to wall studs or other solid surface.

Hauling gardening tools out of the garage every time you want to use them can be a deterrent to getting the work done. A small plastic shed set up near the garden keeps the tools close at hand. A shed like the one shown at right can also be used for storing children's outdoor toys. To protect the contents, choose a shed with a lockable door.

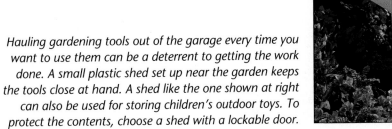

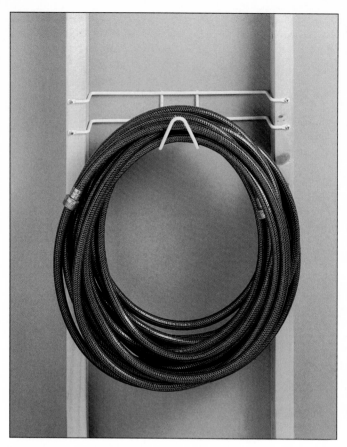

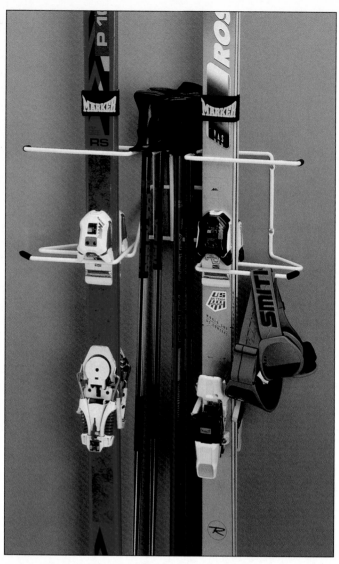

Garden hoses quickly become tangled if they are stored in a haphazard way. A simple rack attached to wall studs (above) will keep a hose neatly looped and accessible.

Skis propped up in a corner can topple over and get damaged. A rack like the one shown at right will keep them upright.

Hanging a bicycle on a rack saves valuable floor space and prevents the bike from falling over. The rack shown at right features a small shelf for storing cycling supplies. Be sure to fasten the rack to wall studs or a solid surface.

The wire rack shown at left provides ample room for storing laundry supplies in the often-overlooked space above a washer and dryer. The rack's freestanding design makes fastening to the wall unnecessary and the small bracket for hanging clothes is a handy accessory.

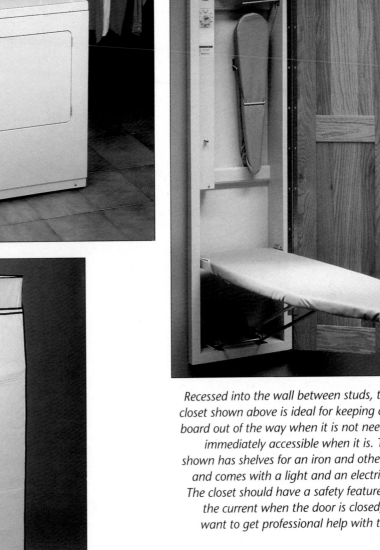

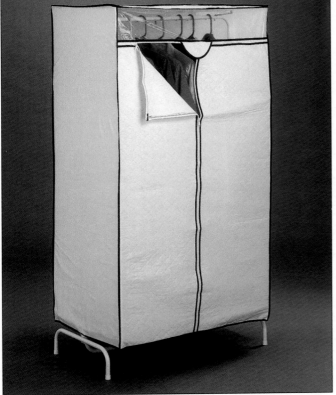

Recessed into the wall between studs, the special closet shown above is ideal for keeping an ironing board out of the way when it is not needed—and immediately accessible when it is. The model shown has shelves for an iron and other supplies, and comes with a light and an electrical outlet. The closet should have a safety feature that cuts the current when the door is closed; you may want to get professional help with the wiring.

Portable garment racks are a good choice for storing out-of-season clothes. To safeguard fabrics, mothballs or cedar chips can be scattered on the bottom of the bag. Some racks are freestanding (left), while others can be hung from ceiling joists or rafters. A rack on casters can be handy in tight spaces. Look for a model with a heavy-duty zipper.

The simple wire rack shown at left can hold a two-week supply of daily papers. The twine-holder makes it easy to bundle a stack of papers: Simply stretch a length of string across the bottom of the rack before stacking the papers, then cut off what you need.

The wall-mounted can crusher shown at right is handy for compacting cans to reduce the amount of space they occupy in a recycling bin.

Metal utility shelves are durable and warp-resistant—perfect for stocking provisions. For storing breakable jars, choose shelves with lipped edges to prevent containers from slipping off; on some models, simply installing the shelves upside down from their usual position provides a lip. Industrial- and office-storage outlets are often a good source of heavy-duty shelving units.

The bins shown at left will enable you to separate your recyclables if required by your municipality; check which materials can be grouped together. With this vertical stacking system, the bins take up relatively little space.

Made of unfinished wood, the wine rack shown at right is attractive and relatively inexpensive. It holds up to four dozen bottles securely and compactly.

BOOKS, DOCUMENTS, AND PHOTOS

Books, magazines, personal documents, financial records, photographs, and correspondence: No collection grows faster, is more difficult to keep organized, and requires such stable storage conditions. Light, moisture, heat, insects, and poor ventilation are all enemies of stored paper products.

What conditions are ideal? Librarians recommend temperatures between 60°F (16°C) and 75°F (24°C) and humidity between 50% and 60% for storing most papers. With good-quality storage units that permit air circulation, consigning these items to a dry and insulated attic or basement should be fine. For photographs and papers that need to be perfectly preserved, hot attics and damp basements are out—unless you control temperature and humidity *(page 89)*.

If you store paper items in cardboard boxes, the lids or flaps should be loose enough to allow a free flow of air. Pack books and magazines loosely, and check occasionally for signs of dampness or mold. Metal units or units lined with metal will protect paper from insects and rodents. Boxes—whether of cardboard or metal—block out light as well.

Books and magazines should be stored on shelves in a dry area that has a stable temperature; cold spaces are acceptable as long as they're kept dry. Don't place shelves against a wall that hasn't been insulated; set them against furring strips fastened to the wall or place polyethylene sheeting between the wall and shelves *(page 7)*. If your books will be exposed to a lot of light, especially fluorescent or direct daylight, equip the shelves with doors or curtains. Magazines can be stored in slipcover cases or binders, available from publishers or office suppliers.

ASK A PRO

WHAT IS THE BEST WAY TO STORE VIDEOCASSETTES?

Videocassettes should be stored upright in their cases in a cool, dry spot. To avoid accidental erasure, keep the cassettes away from magnetic fields produced by equipment such as speakers and telephones.

Storing files

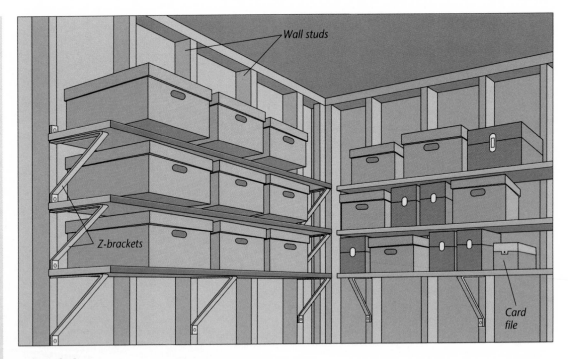

Wall studs

Z-brackets

Card file

Using shelves

An organized collection of cardboard or metal containers for household records, receipts, documents, and correspondence will meet the storage needs of most homeowners. Use individual filing boxes or cartons to handle large items, and canceled check organizers with filing inserts, slipcover letter files, and binding cases for documents. Store bits and pieces of paper in metal and cardboard card files, which are available in many sizes.

Arrange your box system on 1x12 shelves supported by Z-brackets or individual shelf brackets fastened to wall studs. To keep track of what's where, you can number each box to match a corresponding index card listing the contents of the box.

Knee wall

Using file cabinets

A metal file cabinet, with one to five stacked drawers, is a very efficient and safe way to store important documents and photo negatives. To save space, recess the cabinet under stairs *(above, left)* or into a knee wall in the attic *(above, right)* so that only the drawer fronts are exposed. Install a light above the cabinets, as shown. File cabinets are expensive, but you can reduce the cost by purchasing used equipment; look up "Office Furniture and Equipment—Used" in the Yellow Pages.

For maps, oversize documents, and art paper, use wood or steel flat files like the one shown below.

PRESERVING PHOTOS

Although photographic films and papers are more stable and long-lasting today than they were in the past, your photo memories can still fade or discolor if exposed to excessive light, heat, or moisture. Keep them in covered boxes, cupboards, or flat file drawers *(below, left)*. Storage conditions for photo materials must be dry; place a packet of silica gel in each container to help absorb moisture.

Store color slides in boxed projector trays or special clear plastic 8$\frac{1}{2}$x11-inch sheets. Keep black-and-white and color negatives in protective file sheets *(below, right)*; the sheets can then be organized in three-ring binders, which can be kept in a drawer or box. Separate prints with pieces of paper or enclose them in individual rag-paper envelopes, then lay them in flat file drawers or boxes.

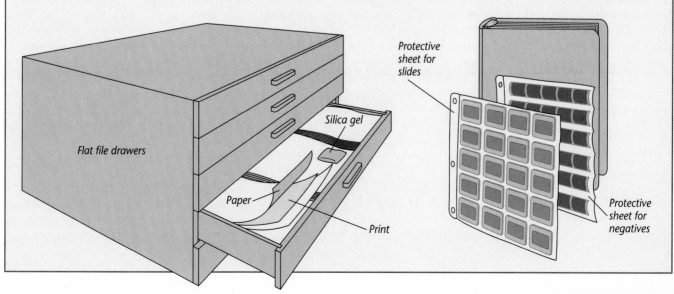

Flat file drawers

Silica gel

Paper

Print

Protective sheet for slides

Protective sheet for negatives

FOOD AND WINE

Basements and crawl spaces stay naturally cooler than the rest of the house in summer and are the ideal spots for storing either food or wine. To keep the area cool when the basement is heated, you may want to consider partitioning off a part of your basement for an insulated food or wine cellar.

FOOD

Household food storage can be divided into two categories: pantry or room-temperature storage for canned goods and nonperishables; and cool root cellar storage for fruits, vegetables, staples, and preserves.

You can store cans and jars just about anywhere that's convenient in the garage or basement—except near a furnace or water heater. Place items on orderly shelves, inside an unused utility closet, or behind cabinet doors. Insect eggs or larvae may be present in dried foods, even if they can't be seen. Keep these foods in rigid containers to confine any insects that may develop.

To create a food cellar in a basement, insulate a small area along a cool basement wall, as shown opposite. Partition off an area adjacent to a shaded north or east wall and away from heating ducts and pipes. If possible, choose a site for your cellar with an outside opening—a window is convenient—to provide air flow. Cool ground temperatures and, when the weather is cool, the outside air will keep cellar temperatures low; the insulation will keep out heated air from the surrounding basement. In a hot climate, the area will be hard to keep cool in the summer. You can consider installing an air conditioner with a thermostat, although this will tend to dry the air. To keep the room moist, set out large pans of water, or spread peat moss or sawdust and dampen it periodically. Wood slats laid on top will keep your feet dry.

An old-fashioned root cellar with a cool dirt floor is another food storage option. Traditionally, root cellars were dug below the house, into the ground outside, or into a hillside. A modern-day crawl space may be just the place to locate your root cellar.

Root crops (except potatoes) require moist, cool storage conditions. Other crops, including potatoes, winter squash, and pumpkins, prefer warmer, drier surroundings (50° to 60°F; 10° to 16°C). Fruits and vegetables should not be stored right next to each other within your storage area: Apples and pears can cause root vegetables to sprout and some vegetables will cause fruits to take on an earthy odor. Consult your local university agricultural extension service for more information about proper food storage. Protect food storage areas against rodents and other animals by keeping the areas clean and screening all openings to the outside.

WINE

If you're serious about wine, you'll soon want an organized, stable environment for your collection. By purchasing young wines or sale wines in bulk, and letting them mature in your own cellar, you'll save the appreciable markup that dealers tack on for each year that wines age on their shelves. Moreover, many fine wines disappear from the market long before they're mature. Remember four factors for successful wine storage: temperature stability, peace and quiet, absence of light, and bottle positioning.

For the optimum aging of wine, it's best to keep the storage area between 50° and 60°F (10° and 16°C); 58°F (14°C) is generally regarded as ideal. Some experts, however, wouldn't pale at the idea of storing wines at room temperature—65° to 70°F (18° to 21°C). Temperature stability is more critical than precise temperature: Wine can tolerate slow temperature changes over a period of weeks, but rapid or extreme fluctuations must be avoided, as they will cause damage.

To control temperature fluctuations or to keep the wine cool, you may want to create an insulated wine cellar in your basement. This can be done in the same way as the food cellar shown opposite.

In addition to temperature fluctuations, wine should be protected from vibration and light. Don't store wine near sources of vibration, such as stairways, washers, and dryers. Sturdy wine racks will help; in earthquake country, bolt your racks to fixed walls.

Direct sunlight and other sources of ultraviolet light may harm wines, so make your cellar lightproof. But don't forget good artificial light for those times when you're hunting for that special bottle or hosting a wine-tasting party.

Wine should always be stored on its side. The cork must be kept moist by the wine inside to prevent air or airborne organisms from entering and spoiling the wine. To help sort out the Beaujolais from the Zinfandel, hang small labels around the necks of the bottles or label each slot in your rack. Keep a complete log of all your wines and their locations.

ASK A PRO

WHERE CAN I KEEP FOOD OR WINE COOL IF I DON'T HAVE A BASEMENT?

Search the house for an area that stays naturally cool; the north side of the house is shadiest. If possible, choose a spot that can be vented to a naturally cool crawl space or outside area.

Keeping food cool

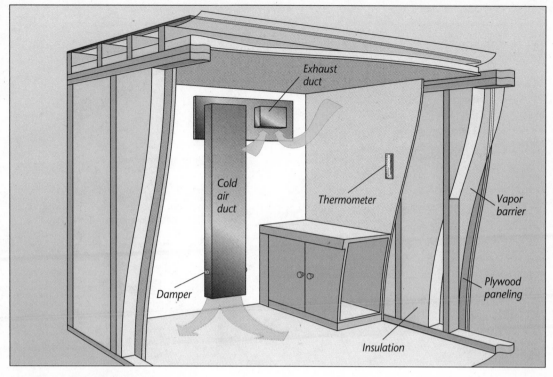

Exhaust duct

Cold air duct

Thermometer

Vapor barrier

Damper

Plywood paneling

Insulation

Creating a food cellar

Once you've chosen a spot for your cellar, insulate the ceiling, new interior walls, the door and, unless the climate is cool year-round, the exterior wall above ground level. As shown above, install a cold air duct with a damper to bring cool air in and a duct with a sliding vent to exhaust warm air to the outside. A fan can be installed in the exhaust duct to blow warm air out. You can control the temperature of the room by opening and closing the damper or turning the fan on and off.

Keeping food within reach

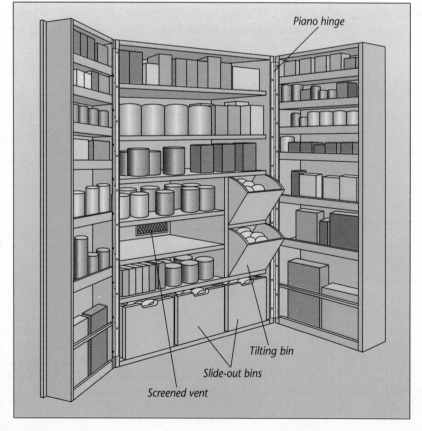

Piano hinge

Tilting bin

Slide-out bins

Screened vent

Building a larder

This built-in larder provides for canned goods, grains, and bulk produce. Screened vents to the outside or a crawl space keep the temperatures low. Deep shelves hold goods; the double doors are lined with narrow lipped shelves that provide more accessible storage. Since the doors are very heavy when loaded, they are attached with piano hinges. The doors can roll on casters, but the unit would have to be raised on a kick base.

Slide-out and tilting bins hold fruits and vegetables. Units similar to the one shown are also available from kitchen cabinet manufacturers.

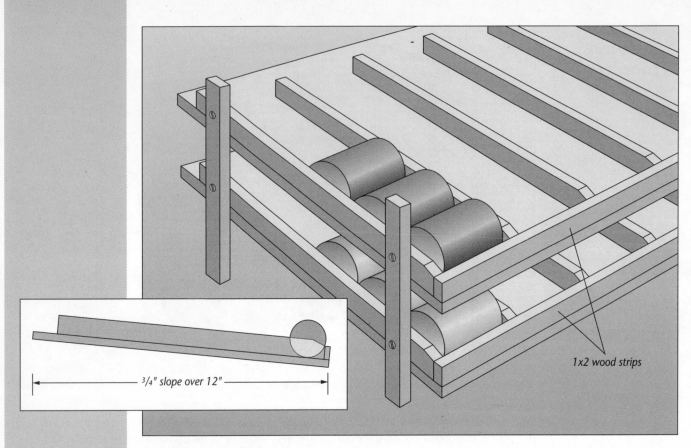

1x2 wood strips

³/₄" slope over 12"

Building sloping shelves

Food shelves that hold only bulk canned goods can be sloped forward so that cans will roll to the front—saving you the trouble of digging for buried cans. Fasten 1x2 strips across the front and sides of the shelves to form channels that keep cans aligned, as shown above. Make the channels ¹/₈" wider than the height of the cans you're storing and, if possible, leave the back of the shelves accessible for loading. The shelves should slope ³/₄" for every 12" of shelf width *(inset)*.

BE PREPARED: EMERGENCY SUPPLIES

If you live in an area subject to natural disasters—floods, earthquakes, tornadoes—you should store emergency supplies in your home. Keep the supplies in a satchel or backpack that you can take with you if you need to evacuate. You should have enough food and water for your household for three days. Food can include canned and dried foods and powdered milk. Most canned goods have a shelf life of about a year so rotate them into your general food storage on a regular basis. You should have at least one quart of water per person per day. Water should be replaced every six months. Keep a pipe wrench or open-end wrench near the gas and water mains to shut the valves.

In addition to food and water, keep the following emergency supplies on hand:
• Portable radio
• Flashlight

• Extra batteries for radio and flashlight
• Whistle to attract attention
• Candles and waterproof matches
• First aid kit and instructions
• Medications needed by family members and, if applicable, special needs for babies and invalids
• Hygiene items—soap, toothpaste, toilet paper
• Metal can with tight-fitting lid or plastic garbage bags; either can be used to store human waste if sewage lines are damaged
• Extra clothing and walking shoes
• Blankets or sleeping bags
• Utensils, paper plates and cups
• Manual can opener
• Portable stove; charcoal should be used outdoors only and butane should not be used until it's determined that there's no gas leak in the area.

Building wine racks

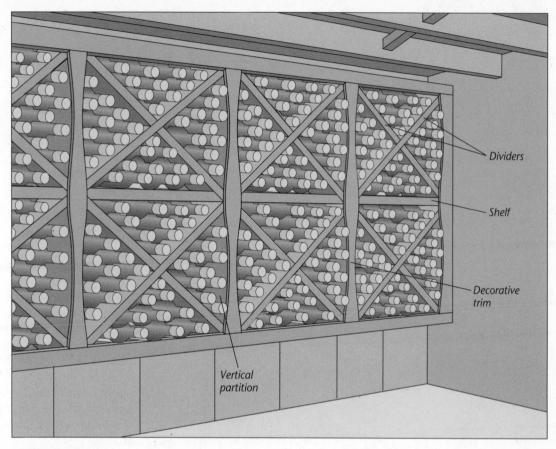

Labels: Dividers, Shelf, Decorative trim, Vertical partition

Triangular bins

For the bins shown above, build vertical partitions, then divide each section with a shelf made of two layers of ³/₄" plywood or 2-by lumber. Cut diagonal dividers of the same thickness to span the compartments from corner to corner and join them with edge half laps *(page 76)*. Cover the exposed edges of the partitions with decorative trim. You can design the bins to hold about one case each.

Vertical slots

The slot system illustrated at right organizes bottles in vertical rows; the bottle sitting in the platform on top displays the contents of each slot below. A 4' high unit will allow each row to store a case of wine.

Assemble the platform from a piece of ³/₄" plywood, with two lips made of 1x3s; make semicircular cutouts to fit the bottle necks every 4" along the front lip.

Cut slats from 1x3s, shaping them at the top so that bottles will slide up and out. Fashion dividers from 1x10s or ³/₄" plywood. Nail the slats against the front edges of the dividers, then fix the platform to the slats and dividers, centering each slat between two semicircular cutouts in the lip, as shown. Nail a plywood base to the bottom of the slats and dividers.

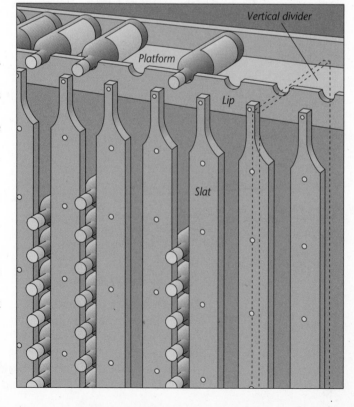

Labels: Vertical divider, Platform, Lip, Slat

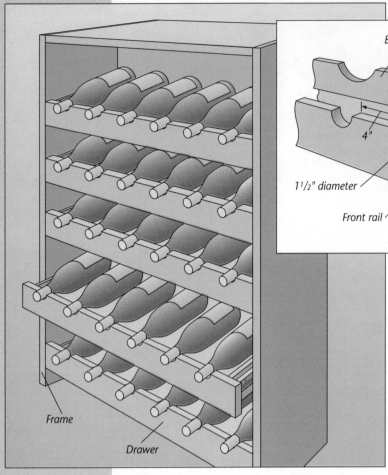

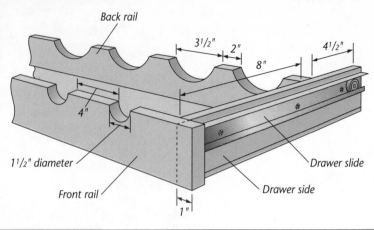

Back rail

$3^{1}/_{2}$" 2" $4^{1}/_{2}$"

8"

Drawer slide

4"

$1^{1}/_{2}$" diameter

Front rail

Drawer side

1"

Frame

Drawer

Sliding drawers

The handy rack shown at left is like a chest of open drawers for wine. Start by shaping the front and back rails from 1x4s as shown in the inset, then connect them with plywood sides and add a bottom. Build a frame for the drawers from 3/4" plywood and fasten it to a wall or the ceiling for stability. Mount the drawers inside the frame with commercial slide runners, attaching the slides to the drawer sides and the runners on the inside of the frame. The drawers shown are 14" deep; they shouldn't be more than about 4' wide.

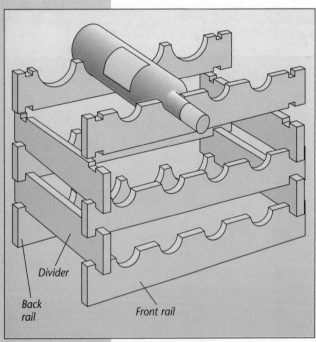

Divider

Back rail

Front rail

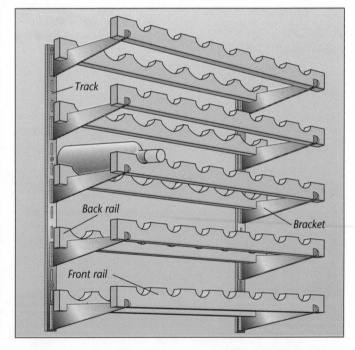

Track

Back rail

Bracket

Front rail

Racks that stack and hang

You can build simple wine racks by shaping boards as you would for sliding drawers (above, top), and then stack the racks or mount them on shelf hardware. For a stacking rack (above, left), cut dividers to separate the rails, and join the rails and dividers with edge half-lap joints (page 76). For a shelf-mounted rack (above, right), install a track-and-bracket shelf system on the wall (page 84), then cut notches in the bottom edges of the rails to fit on the brackets.

READY-TO-USE WINE STORAGE UNITS

The products shown on this page can be used for quick and easy wine storage.

Square chimney flue tiles

To hold square chimney flue tiles in the diamond pattern shown above, build a case to fit tightly around them.

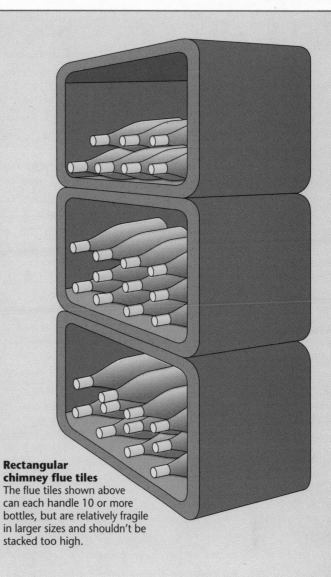

Rectangular chimney flue tiles

The flue tiles shown above can each handle 10 or more bottles, but are relatively fragile in larger sizes and shouldn't be stacked too high.

Drainpipes or mailing tubes

The tubes shown below pigeonhole individual bottles. Set on shelves and contained between concrete blocks, the tubes can be stacked. You can also store bottles on shelves without the tubes, but it will be harder to get at the bottles on the bottom.

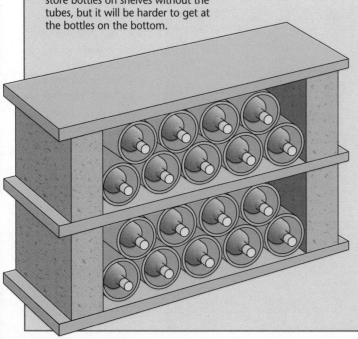

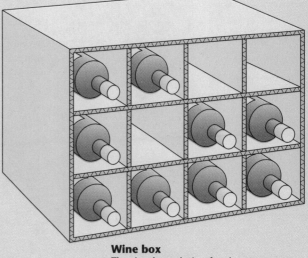

Wine box

The simplest solution for short-term storage is to turn a divided cardboard wine box on its side (above). However, these are not strong enough to be stacked.

RECYCLING

Recycling is a relatively new responsibility for many of us, but it's easy enough when you're organized. First, you should phone your municipality and find out what materials can be recycled in your area as well as what sorting and preparation is required. Usually, certain types of glass, metal, paper, and plastic containers can be recycled. Often, these materials must be separated, while in some areas, no sorting is required. In some areas, plastic bags and milk and juice cartons can also be recycled. The preparation required will vary with the municipality. In general, cans and bottles must be rinsed. In some areas, labels and caps must be removed from bottles and staples must be removed from paper products.

Place both garbage cans and recycling bins in any well-ventilated area protected from the elements: a corner just inside the garage door, a carport enclosure, or a small outdoor shelter beside your home or in the backyard; check local building codes before constructing. For convenience, cans and bins shouldn't be too far from either the kitchen or the driveway or street. Bins should be lightweight and made of plastic, metal, or painted plywood. An easy-to-carry container located in or near the kitchen will save you extra steps until you have a full load.

ASK A PRO

HOW CAN I SAVE ROOM IN MY RECYCLING BINS?

Soft drink cans normally take up a lot of room, but crushing them before putting them in the bins will enable you to store them more compactly. Build a simple can masher from two lengths of 2x4 joined by a heavy-duty butt hinge. You can fashion a round handle at the front end of one pivoting 2x4, and you may want to fasten the device to a wall to keep it steady.

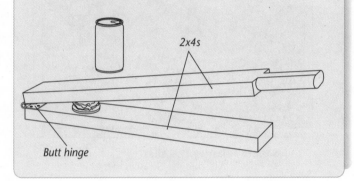

2x4s

Butt hinge

Hanging recycling bins

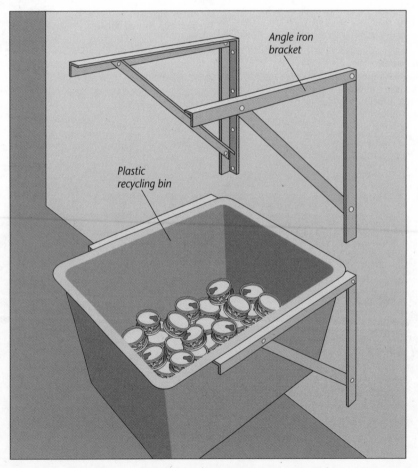

Angle iron bracket

Plastic recycling bin

Wall brackets

Hang plastic recycling bins one above the other to save space. On recycling days, the bins easily slide forward and out. The brackets shown at left are made of angle iron, cut to length and reinforced with diagonal braces bolted in place. The bins will be quite heavy when full, so you should only hang them this way from a solid wall such as plywood or masonry, or if you can find bins whose width corresponds to the spacing between studs. You can also attach drawer guides or runners inside an open cabinet frame to hold bins *(page 49)*. Or for a more finished look, try a commercial stacking bin system.

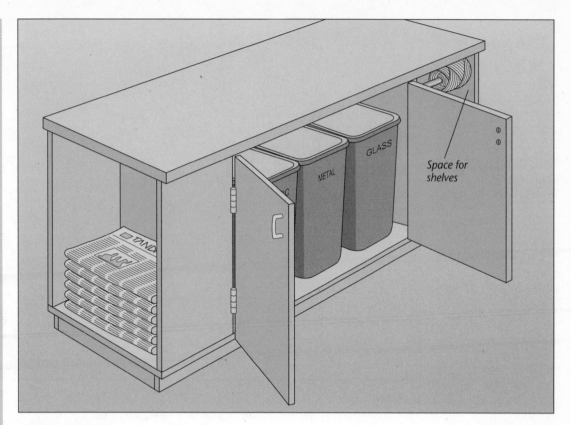

Plywood cabinet

The cabinet shown above provides space for newspapers and plastic recycling bins. A rod holds string for tying newspapers and there's space on the right—under the string—for shelves to hold garbage bags and supplies.

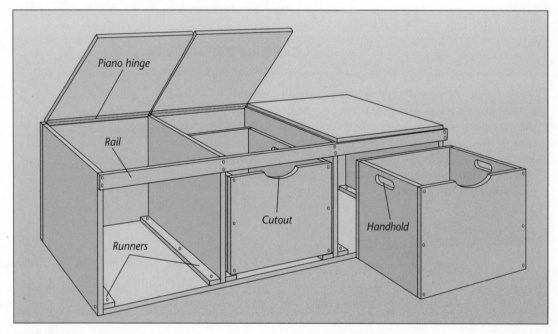

Sliding bins

The enclosed three-bin recycling system shown above can be modified for special needs. Side-by-side bins resting on runners hold recyclable materials that must be separated. Construct the lids and bins from 1/2" exterior-grade plywood; the case from 3/4" plywood; the rail from 1x4 stock; and the runners from 1x2s. Use piano hinges to attach the lids to the back panel.

Flip the lids down to double as counter space or leave them open for easy access to the bins. On recycling days, slide each bin out by gripping the cutout on the front.

Storing newspaper

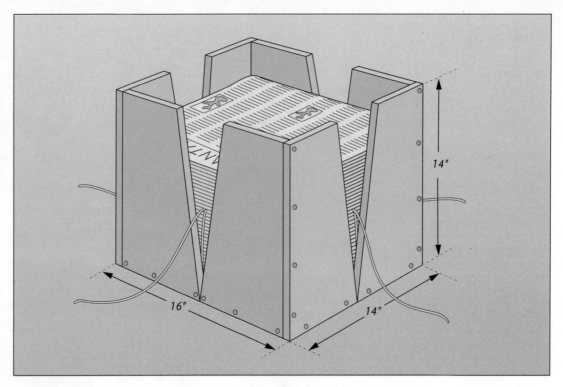

Building a box

Make a box from 3/4" plywood to fit around your newspaper—usually 14" by 16". The box shown above is 14" high, but you can customize your holder to store a week's worth of daily papers. Join the sides using glue and nails. Remember to lay a length of string across the bottom before stacking the papers. Bundle the papers when the box is half full, then lay a new string across the stack, as shown.

GARBAGE DAY MADE EASY

To simplify the chore of lugging heavy garbage cans out to the curb and back, mobilize them on a wagon. Cut the base from 5/8-inch plywood large enough to hold two cans. Make the lip by assembling a frame of 2x4s and attaching them around the perimeter of the base. Finally, fasten heavy-duty casters to the underside of the base at each corner of the wagon.

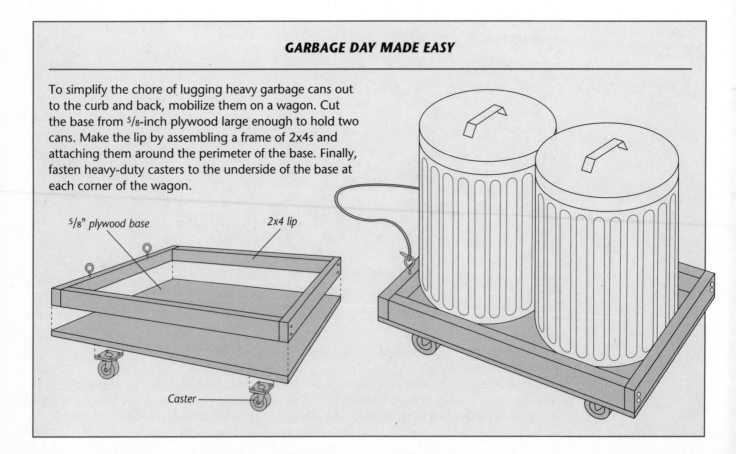

5/8" plywood base

2x4 lip

Caster

FIREWOOD

To an increasing number of people, firewood has become an important supplement to other energy sources which are expensive and sometimes in short supply. In many cases, it is being used as the primary alternative to these more costly sources.

If you buy dry, seasoned wood, you'll need to keep it dry, and if you buy unseasoned wood—lumber that has been recently felled—you'll need to season it by drying. Depending on the species, it can take anywhere from 15 days up to a full year for freshly harvested wood to dry. In both cases, the wood should be stored in such a way that air can circulate around it, while at the same time it is protected from rain, snow, and ground moisture. Wood stored outdoors should be kept off the ground and be sheltered under a shed roof. But, don't seal it off completely because you'll trap moisture and condensation inside the wood. If you split the wood before stacking it, the pieces will dry faster.

Wood can be stacked in parallel or perpendicular (crisscross) rows. For safety and neatness, tall woodpiles should be braced with vertical supports.

ASK A PRO

HOW DO I PREVENT INSECTS FROM COMING INTO THE HOUSE WITH MY FIREWOOD?

Firewood can be infested with anything from ants to wood beetles. Keeping the wood off the ground can help prevent this. Never store wood up against your house. Insects can make their way into the house through cracks in the foundation; at least 10 feet away is ideal. Before bringing wood inside, check it for insects and get rid of as many as possible by banging the wood against the ground.

To reduce the risk of insects spreading once inside the house, only bring in wood as you need it; in general, don't store more than about a day's worth of wood inside. As an additional precaution, you can surround the wood bin inside with sticky glue strips (available at your hardware store) to catch any insects that try to wander away from the wood; glue strips are more effective than bait traps, which only attract certain types of insects.

Storing firewood

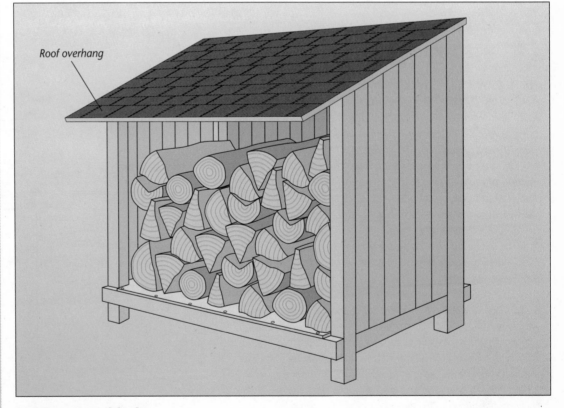

Roof overhang

Building a woodshed
Build a woodshed *(above)* with pressure-treated lumber. Raise the firewood off the ground and leave the shed open on one side so that air can circulate. A roof overhang will keep rain and snow off. CAUTION: Never cut pressure-treated wood indoors and don't burn it. Wear safety glasses and respiratory protection when cutting it, and long pants and sleeves and chemical-resistant gloves when handling it.

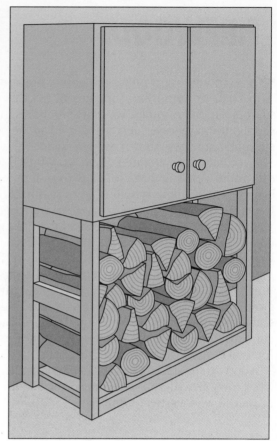

Finding nooks and crannies for firewood

Survey your garage, basement, or carport for likely places to store firewood. A supply of wood can usually be stashed under basement stairs *(above)* or beneath a carport or garage cabinet *(right)*.

 ASK A PRO

HOW CAN I SAVE STEPS FROM THE WOODPILE TO THE FIREPLACE?

Installing a simple wood box through a wall to the outside with an access door near your fireplace can shorten your trips from the woodpile. The door will enable you to pass logs through from the outside instead of making several trips through the house. The opening can be an attractive addition to the room, with a hinged door and a molded frame that projects from the interior wall.

If the wood box opens into a garage or carport, most building codes require that the opening have a solid-core self-closing door. If you live in a cold climate, insulate and weather-strip the door. To keep insects out of the living quarters, line the wood box with sheet metal.

For a stylish variation on this pace-saving idea, store your wood under a fireside bench seat that can be loaded from the outside; when you need a log, just lift the hinged seat. You can also set up a basement-to-fireplace dumbwaiter operated by cables and a hand winch to bring logs to the main floor. Make sure the mechanism is sturdy enough to carry the weight of the firewood.

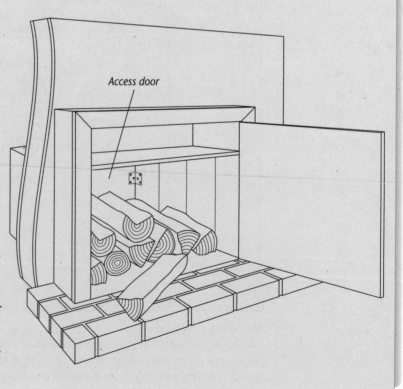

WORKSHOP

A safe workshop should be well organized and properly lit, and have adequate electrical wiring and outlets. (For information on avoiding storage hazards in your workshop, turn to page 16.) You'll need to have plenty of storage space to keep tools and hardware out of the way when you're working, but accessible when you need them.

The focus of your workshop should be a large, stable workbench. Many kinds are available pre-made, but you can make your own from a 2x4 frame with a plywood or hardboard top. The area beneath a workbench is ideal for drawers, cabinets, boxes, and shelves.

Related tools and materials are best grouped together so that you can find them easily. Large power tools mounted on casters can be rolled out from a storage closet or cabinet, or away from a wall, then back again when the work is done. Wall cabinets are best for portable power tools because they protect the blades and working parts from damage and keep them out of

the reach of children. See page 16 for more information on childproof storage.

Hand tools can be a challenge to store properly. The popular perforated hardboard (Peg-Board) and hanger system is best suited for visible, hands-on storage. You can also buy individual wall racks for small tools like screwdrivers and pliers. Though less accessible, closed units like the one shown below protect tools from rust and dust; tools should also be oiled to help prevent rusting.

Besides tools and projects in progress, you'll want to store materials. Leftovers can be stored in a rolling box with a hinged top. Shelf brackets fastened to every other wall stud will handle light lumber. For heavier loads, you can build a lumber rack like the one shown on page 47. Other ideas that can be adapted to storing plywood are shown on pages 62 and 63. Tough fiber storage tubes help protect lengths of pipe or moldings. If you're pressed for space, look to the rafters or ceiling joist.

Designing workshop storage

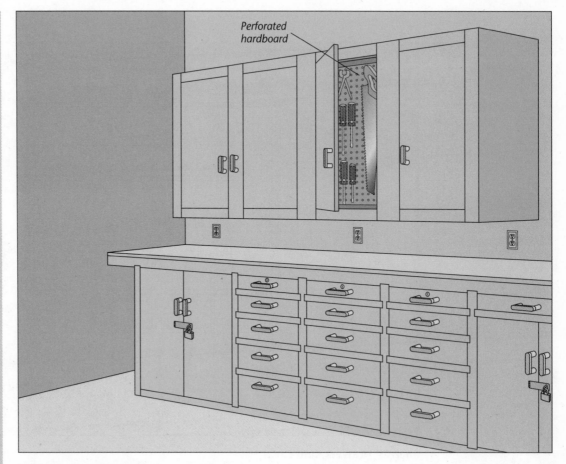

Perforated hardboard

Cabinets and drawers

The storage system shown above combines both cabinets and drawers with a work surface. The cabinets are lined with perforated hardboard for hanging tools; doors shield the tools from dust. The drawers and lower cabinet doors can be locked. The electrical outlets just above the countertop are handy for plugging in power tools.

Less-often-used storables, such as paint, brake fluid, and turpentine, can go on high shelves installed on the wall or suspended overhead or between ceiling joists. In an earthquake area, however, keep flammable liquids low—in a locked cabinet if there are children around. Size and space the shelves to fit the containers and make sure that their labels are visible.

Drawers are a blessing to any workshop owner. Build them into your work counters or in an open frame, or recycle old bedroom dressers or kitchen units. Drawers can hold a variety of small tools and supplies.

For hardware, you'll want small jars, boxes, or bins to hold each type of nail, screw, and washer. You can indicate the containers' contents as shown on page 49.

as shown on page 49.

ASK A PRO

HOW CAN I STOP HOOKS FROM PULLING OUT OF PERFORATED HARDBOARD?

Hooks have a tendency to pull out each time you remove or replace a tool. To prevent this, you can glue the hooks in place by applying adhesive to the end of each one with a glue gun. Of course, this means you can't easily change the layout of the hooks on the board. A more flexible solution is to use small plastic clips (right). Available at your hardware store, these fit over the hooks and lock them to the holes on each side. The clips can be pried off with a pocketknife if you wish to move the hooks.

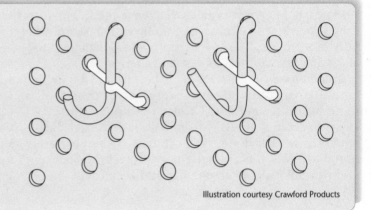

Illustration courtesy Crawford Products

Building a tool cupboard

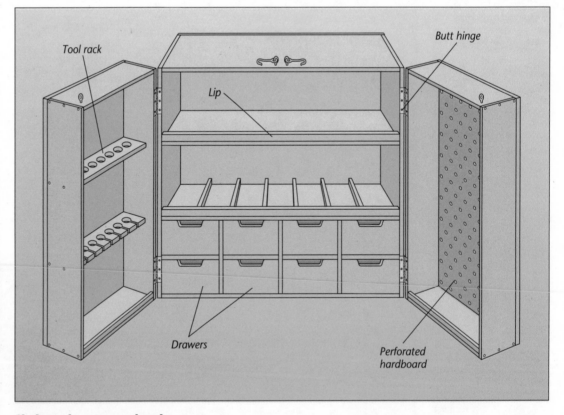

Tool rack

Butt hinge

Lip

Drawers

Perforated hardboard

Shelves, drawers, and racks

The cabinet shown above features double doors for storing hand tools and a main compartment with shelves for small power tools and drawers for supplies. Use the tool rack in one door to hold chisels and screwdrivers, and the perforated hardboard panel in the other door for hanging a hammer or saw. The lip along the front edge of each shelf prevents items from sliding off. Build the case from 3/4" plywood and attach the doors with butt hinges. The unit can sit on a workbench or be hung from wall studs.

HOW DO I KEEP HAND TOOLS IN ORDER?

To make sure each tool goes back in its place on the wall, use silhouettes, as shown at right. The simplest way to make silhouettes is to hang your tools in the ideal order and outline each one with a broad-tipped indelible felt pen. Or, lay each tool on heavy white paper and trace its outline. Then cut out the silhouette and glue it to the wall. The glued-on silhouettes will last longer if you apply a coat of clear sealer over them.

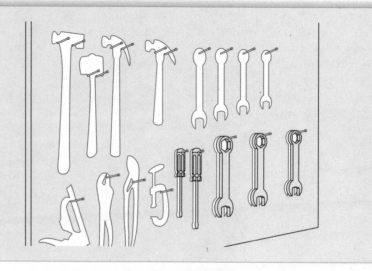

Keeping hand tools handy

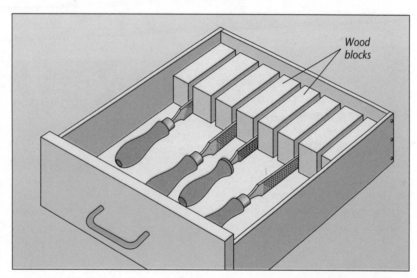

Wood blocks

Drawer dividers

To organize tools in a drawer and protect their edges, cut a series of wood blocks and screw them to the drawer bottom from underneath. Cut the blocks so a portion of the tool blades will be visible and space them to fit the blades *(left)*.

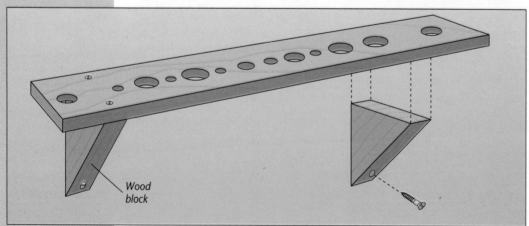

Wood block

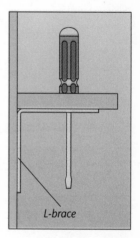

L-brace

Wall-mounted tool rack

A length of 1x3 stock with holes drilled though it makes an ideal rack for hanging tools like screwdrivers and chisels.

Size the holes to fit the tool blades without allowing the handles to slip through. Fasten the rack to the wall with triangular wood blocks cut from 2x4 stock, screwing one edge of the blocks to the underside of the rack and an adjoining edge to the wall *(above, left)*. Alternatively, you can fasten the rack to a wall with L-braces *(above, right)*.

Storing bar clamps

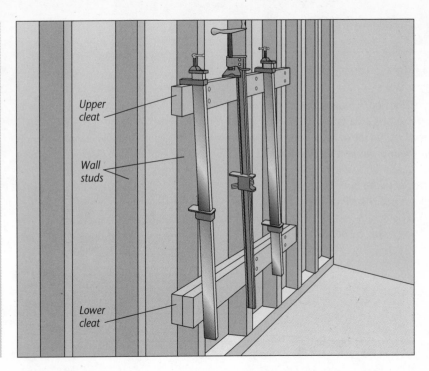

Upper cleat

Wall studs

Lower cleat

Building a wall rack
An unfinished basement wall is an ideal space for storing bar clamps. Nail two cleats cut from 2x4 stock across the wall studs, positioning the upper one high enough to hold the clamps off the floor. Use a pair of 2x4s for the lower cleat to tilt the top of the clamps toward the wall. To store pipe clamps, you can use broom holders *(page 78)*.

Storing blades and bits

Circular saw blades
Protect circular saw blades in a shelved box *(right)*. Build the box from $3/4$" plywood. Before assembling the box, cut $1/4$" wide dadoes *(page 77)* across the sides to accommodate the shelves. To tilt the shelves toward the back and prevent the blades from sliding out, angle the dadoes downward from front to back. Cut the shelves from $1/4$" plywood and slide them into the box.

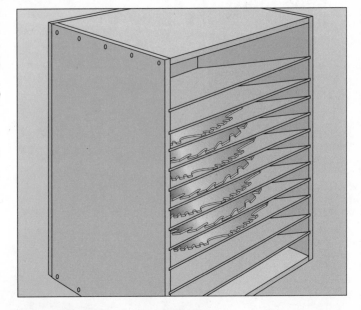

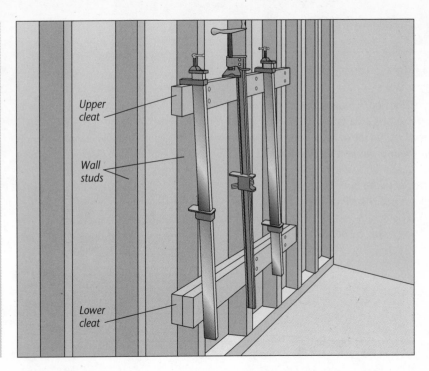

Wood block

Drill or router bits
Drill holes into a wood block to store bits and keep them visible *(left)*. Size the holes to fit the bit shanks snugly and space them so the bits will not touch each other and get nicked. Screw the block to a wall, making sure the fasteners do not intersect with holes for the bit shanks.

Storing wood

Building a rack for lumber and plywood

The rack shown below is designed to hold both boards and plywood. Lumber is stored on the shelves while plywood can be stacked in the channel and secured by the rope.

Cut the frame pieces from 2x4 lumber, making the verticals long enough to span from floor to ceiling, since they must be anchored with bolts to the joists. Bolt the frame pieces together, then fasten the cleats—cut from 1x4 stock—to the front edges of the vertical pieces. The frame pieces can also be joined with half laps *(page 76)*.

Cut the shelves from ³/₄" plywood and fasten them to the top edges of the horizontal pieces. Next, assemble the channel and attach it to the rack. Drill a hole to attach the rope to the front lip of the channel.

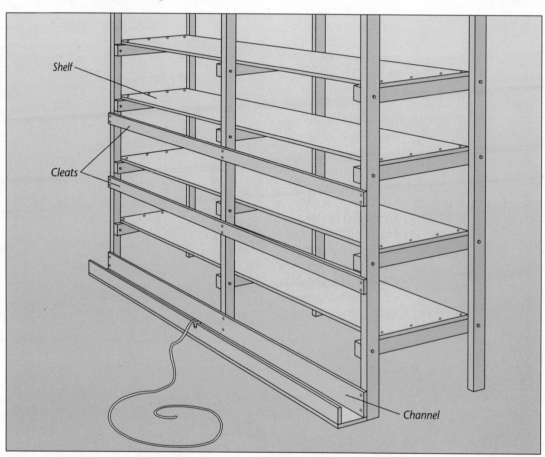

Shelf

Cleats

Channel

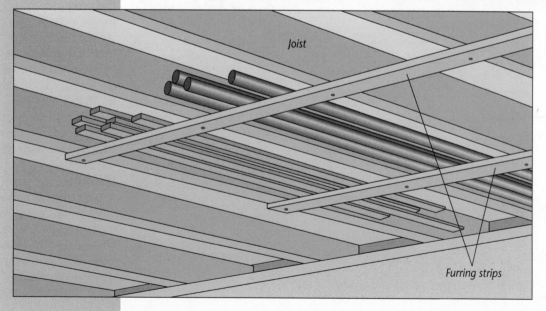

Joist

Furring strips

Using the spaces between joists

Store lumber and lengths of pipe in the gaps between ceiling joists. To fashion these overhead racks, fasten ³/₄" thick furring strips across the bottom edges of the joists with screws, spacing them about 3' apart, as shown. Keep the screws clear of any wires or fixtures running along or through the joists.

Keeping track of hardware

Building a cabinet for hardware bins

The hinged door on the shallow cabinet shown at right flips up to expose a bank of bins. Size the cabinet to fit the number of shelves, vertical dividers, and bins you will be installing. Fasten the door to the cabinet with a long piano hinge, then fix the cabinet to the wall. Label the bins as you fill them.

To hold the door open, attach hooks to the outside of the door and to the ceiling and use a length of chain. Close the door when you're finished with the cabinet to keep out dust. CAUTION: The cabinet on the floor should be kept locked if it contains anything toxic and there are children in the house.

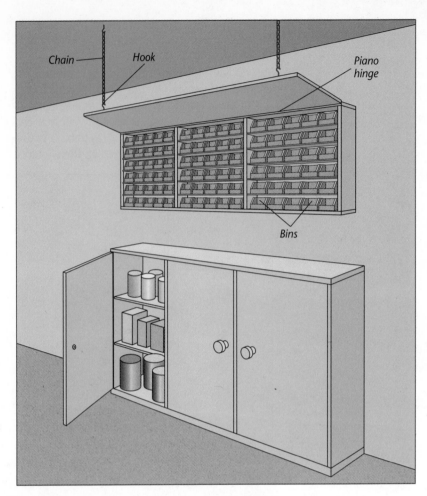

Hanging jars under a shelf

Store fasteners in individual containers, labeling them unless they are glass or transparent plastic. To store jars on a shelf, attach a $1/2$" by $3/4$" lip along the front edge to prevent the containers from toppling off.

Mounting jars under the shelf will double the shelf's storage capacity. Fasten the jar lids to the shelf with screws and washers *(left)*, then screw the jar to the lid.

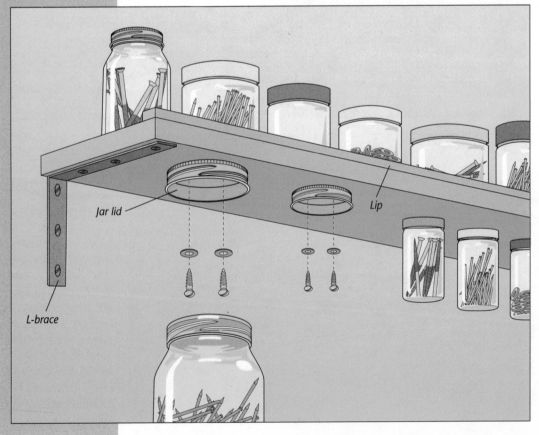

WHAT'S A SIMPLE WAY TO IDENTIFY THE CONTENTS OF BOXES OF FASTENERS?

Although clearly marked labels on containers is a popular option, there's a more effective method. Simply use hot-melt glue to fix a sample of the contents on the outside of the box.

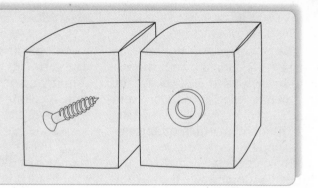

Storing supplies

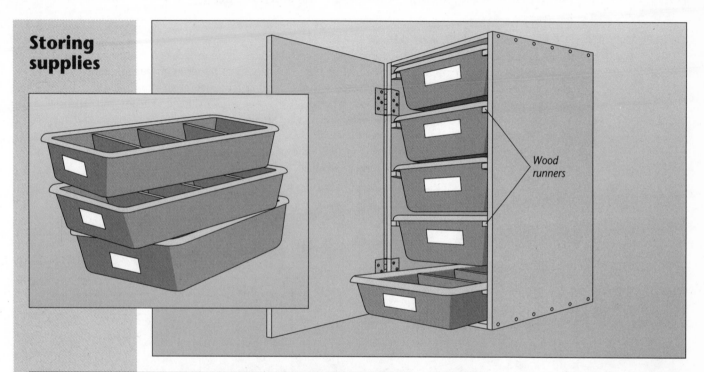

Wood runners

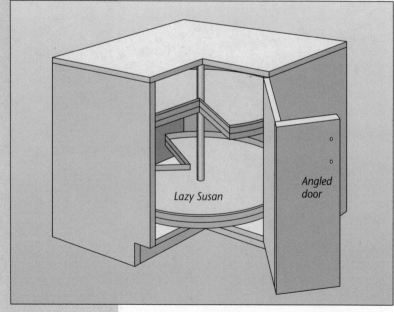

Lazy Susan

Angled door

Sliding bins

Available from office, restaurant, or school suppliers, sturdy plastic bins are ideal for storing supplies. Those shown above are subdivided and have a lip around the top edges, which makes them easy to install inside a plywood cabinet. Fasten wood runners to the inside faces of the cabinet sides, spacing them to fit the bins. Hang the bins on the runners, sliding them in and out as needed.

To protect the contents from dust or simply conceal them, install a door on the cabinet.

Lazy Susan

A lazy Susan—a circular shelf that rotates around a rod—simplifies the task of accessing items in a corner cabinet. You can buy both the lazy Susan and cabinet ready-made. If you decide to build the cabinet yourself, make the door to match the L-shape of the cabinet, as shown at left.

LAUNDRY

Storage units and accessories above and around your washer and dryer make for an efficient laundry area. Place a long deep shelf—or shelves—directly above the machines for frequently used supplies, or consider a commercial unit like the one shown on page 27. Above the shelf is a perfect spot to install ceiling-high cabinets for cleaning supplies, linens, and overflow storage.

Every laundry area needs counter space for folding, sorting, and mending clothes. Plastic laminate counters are easy to clean. In cramped quarters, a fold-down counter is convenient. You may also want a sink for washing delicate garments or soaking out stains. Hang clothes for drip-drying on a metal or wooden closet rod over the sink. A ceiling fan directly above promotes quick drying. A fan is also a good idea to disperse fumes from the soap and bleach.

Install cabinets or large-capacity storage bins below the counter. On the wall, attach a narrow cabinet or a rack for your ironing board. You may want to wall off your laundry area to hide clutter and muffle the noise of machines.

Storing an ironing board

In a closet or dedicated cabinet

A full-size ironing board can be stored near the laundry area either inside a storage closet or in a special shallow cabinet. In a storage closet, secure the board with a chain or strap, or build a narrow slot so that it stands upright *(below, left)*.

If you're building a cabinet for your ironing board, you'll need to buy a fold-down board. Measure the board and allow several inches around it for access.

For extra convenience, add a sleeve board, a clothes hanger, and shelves inside the cabinet as well as an electrical outlet for an iron *(below, right)*.

For simpler storage solutions, you can install an ironing board on the back of a door so that it folds down when needed, or simply fasten a commercially available ironing valet rack to a wall or door to hold the board and iron.

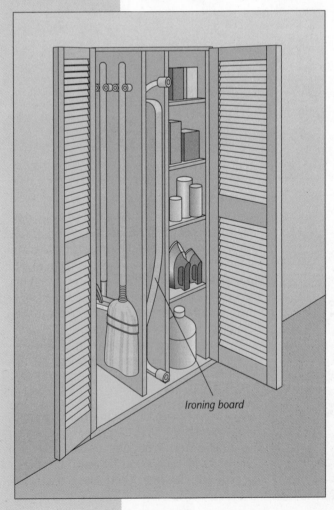

Ironing board

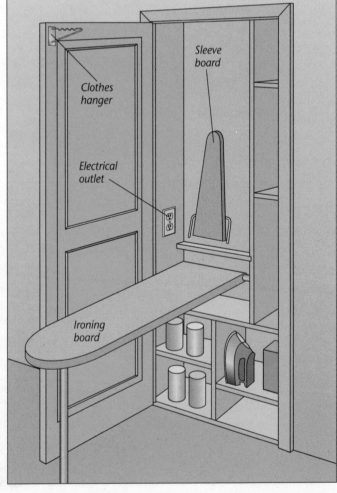

Clothes hanger

Sleeve board

Electrical outlet

Ironing board

Keeping clothes sorted

Using a divided drawer

Two options for sorting clothes for the laundry are shown below. You can build a cabinet with a single deep drawer and partition the drawer with plywood dividers into separate compartments for whites, colors, and permanent press items *(below, top)*. Another divider could be added, creating a compartment for towels or work clothes. Install the drawer with heavy-duty commercial slide runners. Alternatively, buy a commercial sorting tray with individual slide-out bins *(below, bottom)*. For added convenience and mobility, this model has casters.

If you have space under a counter, inside a free-standing island, or against a wall, you can simply stack sorting bins to keep clothes ready to go when laundry day arrives.

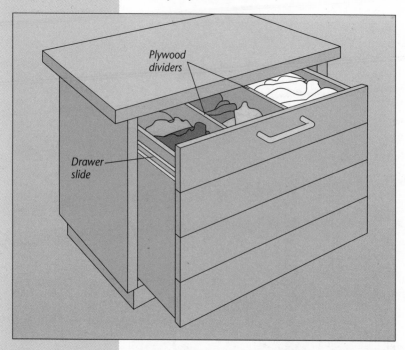

Plywood dividers

Drawer slide

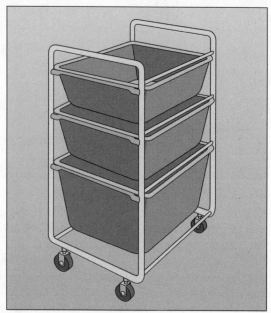

ASK A PRO

WHERE SHOULD I LOCATE A LAUNDRY CHUTE?

A laundry chute directs dirty clothes from your home's main or second floor to a laundry center in the basement or garage below. You can locate the chute opening in an inconspicuous but handy spot—inside a clothes closet in the master bedroom; in a wall, with a hinged or flap door; or inside a bathroom cabinet. If you have small children, be sure that the opening is raised high above the floor or measures no more than 12 inches across.

The best time to construct your laundry chute is when you're designing or remodeling your house. Build the chute from plywood, sheet aluminum, or 18-inch-diameter furnace heating duct.

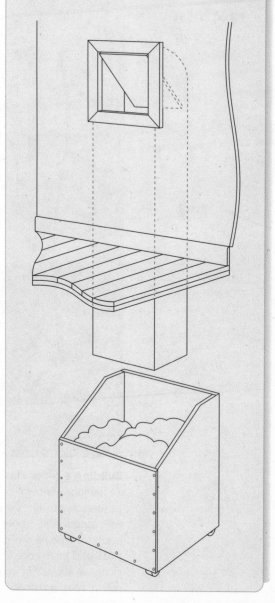

CLOTHING

Stored clothing needs to be protected from moisture, dust, and insects. Moisture, in the form of condensation or actual seepage, is best controlled within the entire storage area; see the chapter beginning on page 89 for remedies. Closed units are valuable where dust or insects are major concerns. Built-ins are the most functional, but portable clothes closets, such as the one shown on page 27, are a simpler solution.

Although storing clothes in a traditional cedar closet or chest, or using cedar-scented moth-controlling substances in garment bags, chests, or closets, will help deter moths, it will not actually exterminate them. You will have to resort to commercial moth-proofing products, such as mothballs, to kill the moth larvae, but the odor can be unpleasant. For these products to be effective, place them in a tightly enclosed space. Because this can encourage the growth of mildew, some moth-proofing products are combined with a mildew-inhibitor. To prevent mildew in a closed unit where you aren't using mothballs, vent it with finely screened openings. Make sure that clothes are thoroughly clean before storing them, since soilage will attract moths.

Keeping clothes moth-free

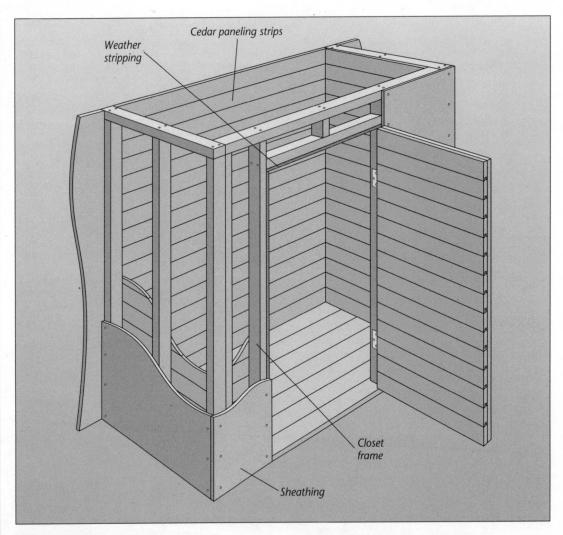

Cedar paneling strips

Weather stripping

Closet frame

Sheathing

Building a cedar closet

To fashion your own cedar closet—or convert an existing closet—line the interior of the closet frame with tongue-and-groove cedar paneling, available in kits from home centers. Cut the strips to length and install them edge to edge, one wall at a time, as shown above. For maximum protection, line the ceiling, floor, and door. Weather-strip the doorway tightly. (If you're building a closet, construct the frame from 2x4s and add 1/2" wallboard or plywood sheathing.)

Don't finish or seal the cedar—you'll lock in the fragrance. To revive the fragrance, sand the surface lightly with fine sandpaper. Turn to page 11 for a way to fit a closet under the rafters in an attic.

Hanging garment bags

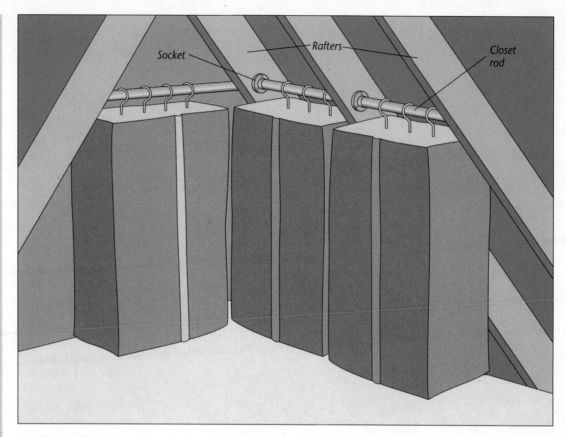

Between rafters

In an attic, hang garment bags from closet rods fastened between the rafters, as shown above. Rather than drilling holes through the rafters—which will weaken them—attach pole sockets to the rafters and fit the rods in the sockets. Garment bags are available in vinyl or fabric in several styles and sizes.

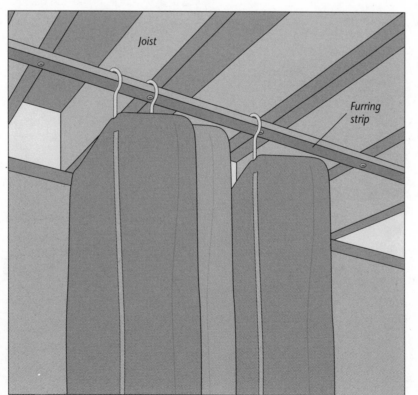

From ceiling joists

In a basement, hang garment bags from 1x2 furring strips screwed across the ceiling joists (left). As with rafters, never bore holes through joists for closet rods.

OUTERWEAR AND SPORTS EQUIPMENT

You may want to rotate sports equipment by season, keeping in-season items close at hand and putting out-of-season ones into less accessible areas. Some sporting goods, such as baseball bats and tennis rackets, can be stored on racks *(page 26)* or perforated hardboard. A stack of deep cubbyhole shelves near the garage door can make camping and fishing gear immediately accessible. Metal school lockers—either new or recycled—are familiar storage units. String simple nylon hammock overhead for basketballs, footballs, and sleeping bags.

To save space, a bike can be hung from a wheel from a bicycle hook *(page 78)*. Men's bikes can also be suspended from the crossbar, as shown on page 58. Floor racks are also a good option, but for winter storage it's a good idea to keep the tires off the ground.

Skis are easily propped up by the pair or grouped in a rack. Turn to page 65 for another ski-storage solution. Snowshoes, skates, and small sleds are best hung on nails, spikes, pegs, or hooks *(page 78)*. Toboggans and bigger sleds can rest atop raised platforms or on ceiling joists or collar beams in the garage.

For outerwear, you may want to design a mudroom in a basement or attached garage. Furnish it with a long bench for removing wet boots and rain pants, and pegs or hooks and a long shelf for parkas, gloves, and hats. Equip the area beneath the bench with drawers or a storage chest for dry socks and shoes. A complete mudroom might include some source of heat—an adjacent water heater or heating duct—to help clothes dry quickly. Make sure the floor can withstand moisture.

Equipping a mudroom

Ledger strips

1x3s

Wire screen

Ledger strips

Support post

Setting up drying racks

Dry items like skates and mitts on shelves. Make the shelves with wire screen or hardware cloth sandwiched in a frame of 1x3s; stagger the joints between the upper and lower frame pieces *(inset)*.

To install the shelves in a corner, attach ledger strips to the adjoining walls and a 2x4 post flush against the unsupported corner of the shelves. Fasten the shelves to the ledger strips and to the support post *(left)*.

To dry shoes and boots, drill angled holes into a 2x10 board and glue in dowels. Fasten the board to the wall *(below)*.

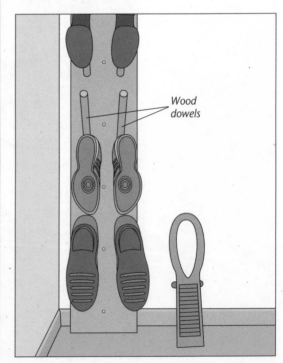

Wood dowels

Storing ski equipment

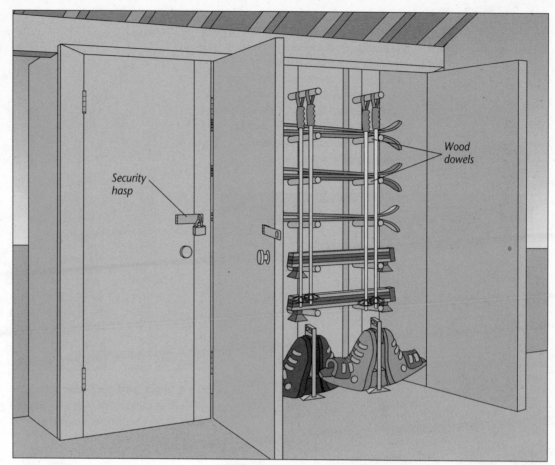

Security hasp

Wood dowels

In a carport
Provided there is sufficient clearance *(page 13)*, a carport is a handy spot for ski equipment. Skis, poles, and a car ski rack rest on dowels in the long, shallow closet shown above. Boots can go on the floor—or inside your house in very cold climates.

For security, choose hinges with fixed pins, attach the hinges to the inside edges of the door and frame, and install a security hasp and padlock on each door.

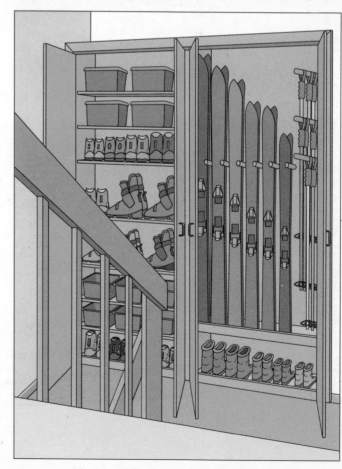

On a landing
Boots and skis for a large family are easy to keep in order in the shallow compartments built on the stairway landing shown at right. Skis are propped up against the back of the closet wall with pegs to keep them from sliding sideways.

Poles are hung from dowels glued into a strip of wood, as shown opposite, which is then attached to the side of the cupboard.

In a pull-down cupboard

An overhead compartment in the space between the joists in a finished basement is a convenient hiding place for ski boots or other gear. Use barrel bolts to keep the compartment closed.

The cupboard shown below is kept from opening all the way by a closet rod; you can also attach a chain between the door and ceiling to hold the door partly open.

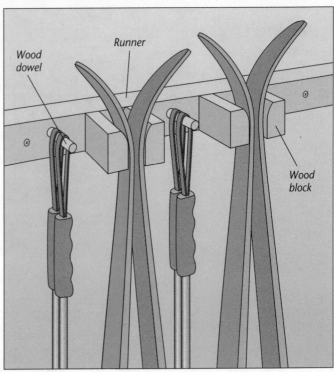

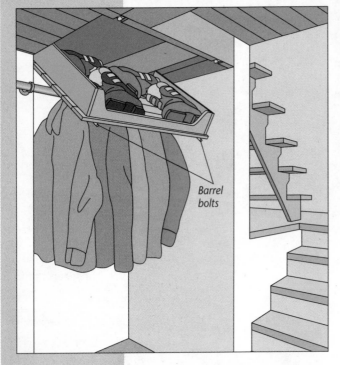

On a block and peg rack

With their curved tips, skis are easy to hang between blocks or pegs. Make the simple rack shown above by fixing a pair of wood blocks to a runner board for every set of skis and fastening the runner along a wall.

Drill pilot holes in 2x4 blocks, then attach them to the 2x4 runner with glue and screws. Space the blocks 1¼" apart, rounding over and sanding their inside edges to follow the profile of the skis and prevent scratching them. Store ski poles by hanging their straps on dowels glued into holes drilled into the runner.

Stashing sleds

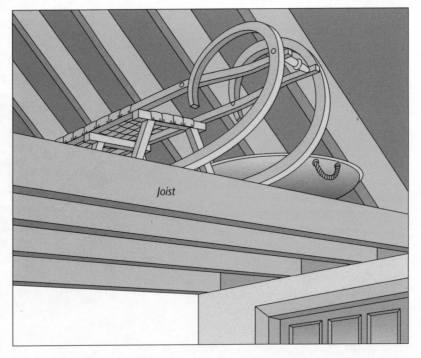

Using the space above joists

In some garages, there's usable storage space between the joists or collar beams overhead and the rafters.

As shown at left, this space provides a ready-to-use storage spot for sleds and other outdoor equipment.

Storing guns

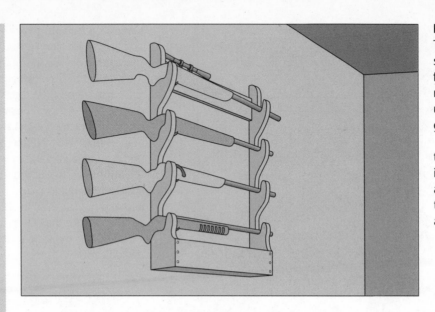

Building a gun rack

The wall-mounted rack shown at left is made from 1-by lumber with notches cut in the uprights to support the gun stocks and barrels.

To store rifles out of the reach of children, install the rack in a lockable room, and be sure to keep the room locked at all times.

PLAY IT SAFE

KEEPING GUNS SECURE

Improper storage of guns leads to accidents. Mishaps typically occur when a firearm is being cleaned, or when a child or burglar finds a gun in the home. Take the following steps to prevent firearm-related accidents and theft:

• For maximum security, keep guns in a locked steel cabinet or gun safe. If your guns are stored in a special room or closet, make sure it is locked; to prevent theft, you can add an interior steel door or curtain. A number of locking devices are available to prevent guns from being fired; these
include trigger locks and locking cables that feed through the triggers.

• Always store guns unloaded and keep the ammunition in a separate, locked location. Store ammunition in its original labeled containers. Guns should be stored in a dry area and ammunition shouldn't be stored near heat sources.

• Make sure everyone in your household knows how to handle the guns safely. Your local police department can help with training programs.

• Teach children that guns aren't toys.

Storing bicycles

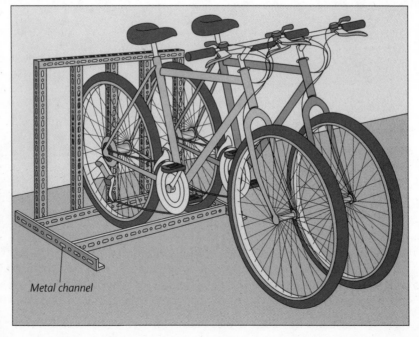

Metal channel

Setting up a floor stand

Bicycle stands like the one shown at left are as convenient at home as they are at school or the park. You can buy a commercial rack or build your own from L-shaped slotted metal channel; assemble the stand using nuts and bolts.

Concrete bike blocks with a slot for the front wheel may be available from building suppliers. These blocks are heavy enough to stay put, but can be moved to suit changing needs.

Installing hanging racks

To hang a bike along a stud wall, fasten closet rod brackets like the one shown to two adjacent studs, then set the bike's crossbar in the notches *(left)*.

To hang bikes from a ceiling joist, build a T-shaped rack as shown below. Cut the vertical supports and brace from 2x4 stock and the crossbar holders from 1x3s. Notch the top ends of the supports to hug a joist and saw half laps *(page 76)* at the bottom ends. Cut round notches into the top edges of the holders, then bolt the supports to the joist and holders. Nail the brace between the supports and place the bike in the crossbar notches. In a garage, size the racks so the bikes won't obstruct parked cars.

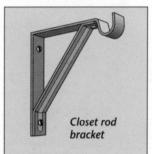

Closet rod bracket

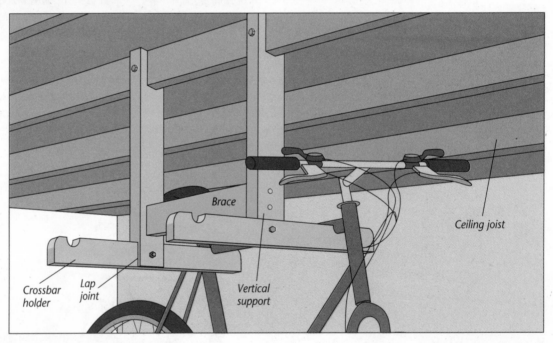

Brace

Ceiling joist

Crossbar holder

Lap joint

Vertical support

ASK A PRO

HOW DO I STORE A BOAT?

Very light boats such as kayaks can be hung from an inside or outside wall in loops of rope. For heavier boats, build a simple rack fastened to garage wall studs. Use lag screws to attach a 2x4 to the side of a stud and then brace it with another 2x4 installed diagonally. Boats can also be hung from joists or collar beams—providing they can handle the weight. If you're unsure, check with a professional. You can also build a cradle with a pulley system (page 63).

FURNITURE AND OTHER BULKY ITEMS

Most furniture, such as dining room tables and over-stuffed chairs, is much too heavy or awkward to fit into standard storage units. You may be able to get lighter furnishings up onto overhead platforms, but the best approach to storing furniture is to keep it out of the traffic flow—in attic or basement corners and against walls—and arrange the pieces as compactly as possible. For furniture in long-term storage, consider renting a storage locker to free up space at home.

Protect furniture by covering it with old mattress pads or blankets. Polyethylene sheeting, canvas, or even newspaper can also help keep dust off. Lamps, decorations, and breakables should be stored on heavy-duty shelves.

Hang lightweight objects, such as outdoor furniture and folding chairs, on garage or basement walls, or place them on a loft platform or overhead rack, or inside carport storage units. If possible, store bulky outdoor items in a garden shed, patio storage unit, or garage extension.

To store card or Ping-Pong tables, model train or game boards, and suitcases during the off season, look for out-of-the-way ledges; or build enclosures specially tailored to their dimensions; or construct an overhead platform. With a pulley system, you can even pull an unwieldy table or trunk up out of the way without having to build a platform.

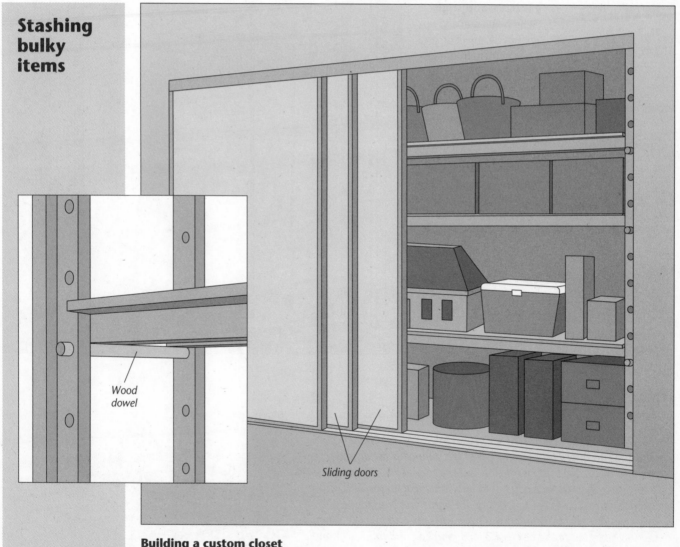

Stashing bulky items

Wood dowel

Sliding doors

Building a custom closet
Bulky, seldom-used belongings call for special storage solutions. The custom-built closet shown above has three sliding doors that open two at a time, accommodating large items. Deep, sturdy shelves can be raised or lowered on adjustable dowels that fit into holes in vertical supports *(inset)*. This design can also be used for open shelving.

Storing carpets and quilts

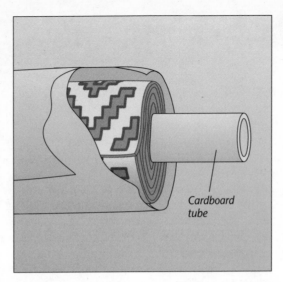

Cardboard tube

Rolling and wrapping

Roll a rug or carpet around a pole or cardboard tube, then loosely wrap the carpet in paper or plastic, leaving some air space *(left)*. Never fold a rug or carpet. Store the carpet in a space that is neither damp nor overly warm; excessive dryness is as harmful as mildew. Use mothballs or crystals to help keep insects away, but keep in mind that some fibers react adversely to these repellents. Consult a carpet expert before storing a prized carpet.

To store heirloom quilts and fine blankets, roll or loosely fold them, then wrap them in clean cotton pillowcases or sheets. Never store a quilt in a plastic bag; the fibers need to breathe. And keep quilts from direct contact with wood. Take your quilts out of their cases occasionally and refold them differently.

Propping up mattresses

Keeping mattresses upright

Store mattresses and box springs off the floor, and prevent them from sagging. Stand them upright against a wall on a plywood base propped up on bricks or blocks. Cover the mattress with plastic or a sheet.

To prevent the mattress from falling over, support it with a sheet of plywood or its own headboard and slats. Fasten eye hooks into the wall, wrap bungee cords around the mattress and attach them to the eyes.

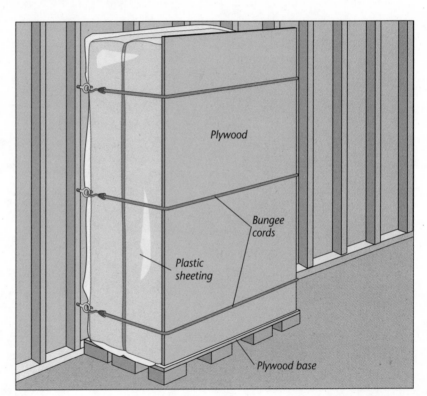

Plywood

Bungee cords

Plastic sheeting

Plywood base

ASK A PRO

HOW DO I KEEP CHRISTMAS LIGHTS UNTANGLED?

Save the cardboard tubes from rolls of gift wrapping paper and a few small-to-medium cardboard boxes. Cut the tubes to fit in the boxes lengthwise, then cut a V-notch into one end of each tube and secure a light strand plug in the notch. Coil the lights firmly around the tubes, as shown at right, by rotating the tube; tape the end in place. Then slip the tubes inside the box; a 12-inch-long box and tube will handle a strand of 35 to 50 small twinkle lights.

You can also wrap lights lengthwise around a long, flat piece of notched cardboard.

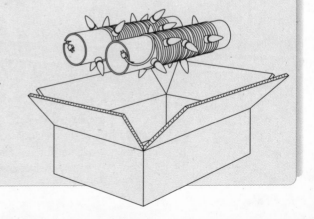

Hanging up furniture

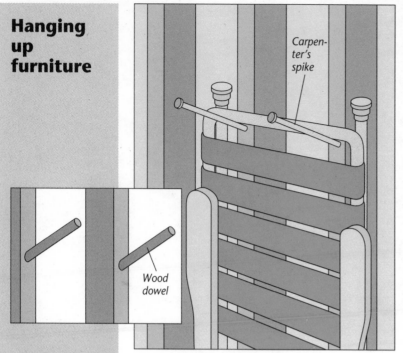

Carpenter's spike

Wood dowel

Shelf bracket

L-brace

Lawn chairs

Save precious floor space by hanging lightweight folding lawn chairs and recliners from wall studs, ceiling joists, or rafters. For simple supports, drive long nails, known as carpenter's spikes, into framing members; use two for each chair *(above, left)*.

You can also drill holes for 3/4" dowels and glue them in *(inset, left)*. Shelf brackets *(above, right)* or L-braces *(inset, right)* will also get the job done. Yet another possibility is a simple track-and-bracket shelving system.

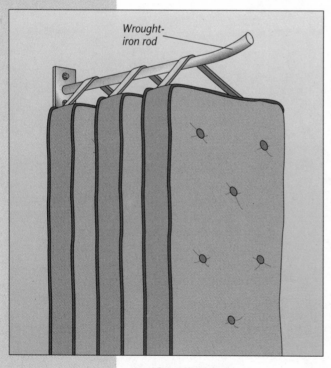

Wrought-iron rod

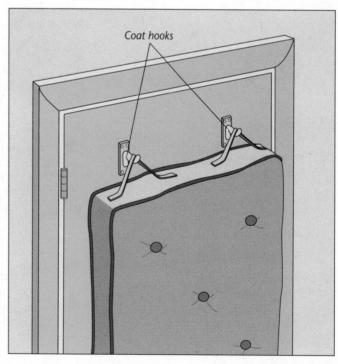

Coat hooks

Outdoor cushions

When bad or cool weather sets in, it's time to bring outdoor furniture cushions inside. Cushions should be stored off the ground to provide good air circulation, which promotes quick drying and prevents mildew problems.

Attach a wrought-iron rod to a wall stud *(above, left)* to hang several cushions from their hand loops or from loops you've sewn in place. You can also mount metal coat hooks on studs or on a closet door to hold individual cushions *(above, right)*.

Building wall racks

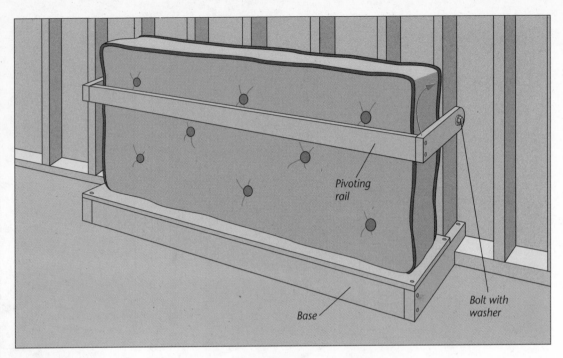

Pivoting rail

Bolt with washer

Base

Pivoting rail

The rack shown above will hold a mattress, or a Ping-Pong or game table. You can keep the object off the floor on a 2x4 base topped with a plywood shelf. For the rail, use 1x3 stock; leave the bolt or lag screw attaching the rail to the studs a little loose so you can pivot it.

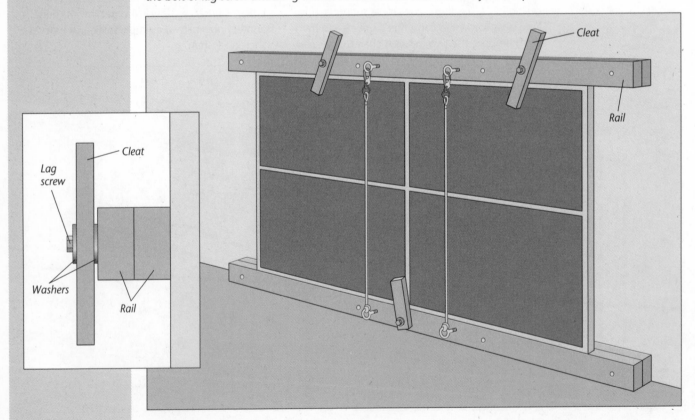

Cleat

Rail

Cleat

Lag screw

Washers

Rail

Swiveling cleats

To hold the top of a ping-pong table or game table against a wall, build a rack like the one shown above. For each rail, nail two 2x4s face to face to the wall; the space between the rails should equal the table width plus 1/4" for clearance.

Cut the cleats from 1x2 stock and fasten them to the rails using lag screws and washers *(inset)*; leave the screws loose enough so you can pivot the cleats. For extra security, attach a pair of ropes between the rails, fastening them to eye screws.

Using pulleys

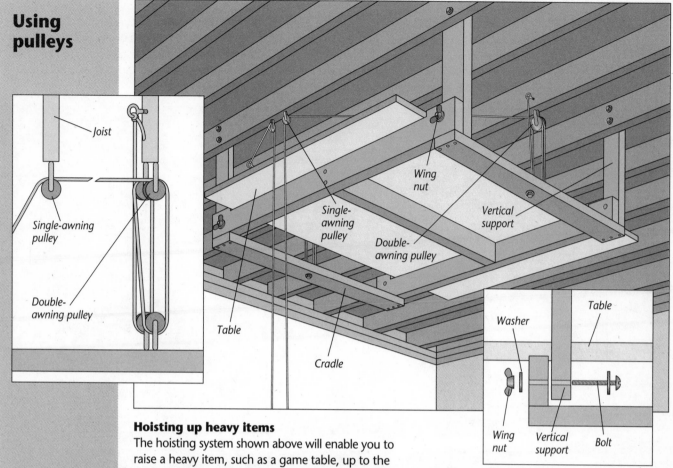

Joist

Single-awning pulley

Double-awning pulley

Single-awning pulley

Double-awning pulley

Wing nut

Vertical support

Table

Cradle

Washer

Table

Wing nut

Vertical support

Bolt

Hoisting up heavy items

The hoisting system shown above will enable you to raise a heavy item, such as a game table, up to the ceiling. Assemble a cradle for the table from 2x4 stock, then use a double-awning pulley—a device with a pair of side-by-side wheels—to link each side of the cradle to the joists. Attach two single-awning pulleys to a joist at one end of the cradle, then feed the hoisting ropes once around each wheel of the double-awning pulleys and over to the single-awning pulley *(left inset)*. Pull on the ropes to hoist the cradle.

Once the cradle reaches the ceiling, anchor the ropes, and use a bolt and wing nut *(right inset)* to attach the corners to vertical supports that are cut from 2x4s and bolted to joists. This will take the weight off the pulleys.

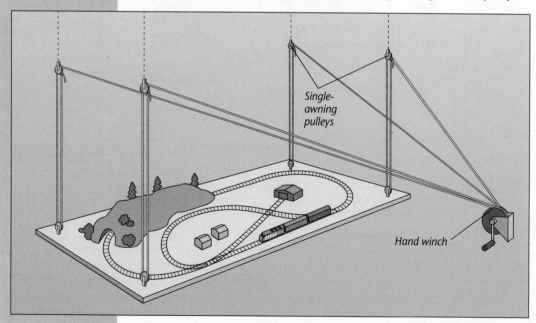

Single-awning pulleys

Hand winch

Raising lighter items

To hoist light items, such as a train board, single-awning pulleys are sufficient. At each corner of the board, use a hoisting rope and two pulleys, attaching one to the board and the other directly above to a joist *(left)*. Raise the board with a hand winch.

Creating storage off the ground

Garage platform

The platform shown below utilizes the space above your car hood in the garage. Cut the posts from 4x4s, the frame pieces from 2x6 stock, and the top from ⅝" plywood. Size the pieces so the posts will straddle the car and the frame will extend above the hood without contacting the windshield *(inset)*. Use nails to assemble the platform, then bolt it to the wall studs or to a masonry wall. You can also use the space above ceiling joists in a garage, as described on page 94.

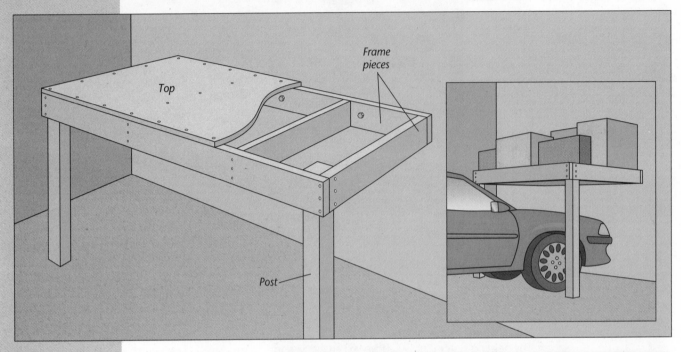

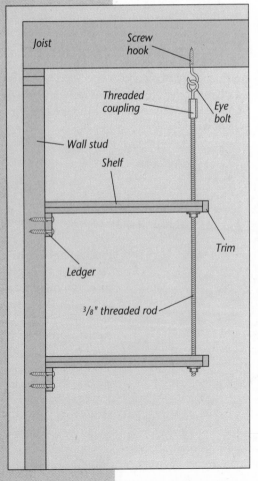

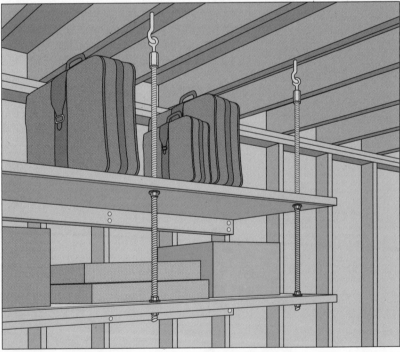

Hanging shelves

Fastened to wall studs and ceiling joists, the shelving shown above can hold heavy items. Make the shelves by gluing two ¾" plywood panels together; you can conceal the front edges by gluing on solid-wood trim. To support the shelves at the back, use 1x4 ledgers, screwing them to every second stud. For the front, drill a ⅜" diameter hole through the shelf at every second joist, feed a threaded rod through the holes, and attach the rods to the joists *(left)*.

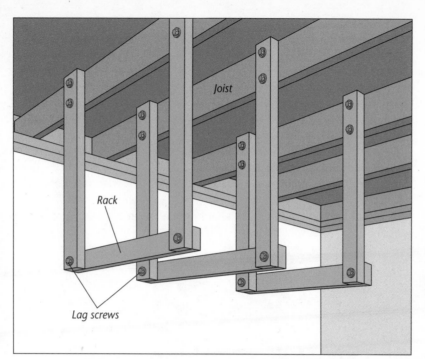

Joist

Rack

Lag screws

Ladder shelves
U-shaped racks made from 2x4 stock and attached to ceiling joists *(left)* are handy for keeping storm sashes, screens, window shades, and ladders out of the way.

Assemble the racks with lag screws or bolts, then bolt the uprights to the joists; use nails or screws for lightweight storage. Or, you can use half-lap joints instead of the simple butt joints shown. To store storm windows compactly, offset their hardware as you stack them.

Finding hidden space

Behind a cabinet
To slide narrow items like chairs or tables in and out of the back of a cabinet, install a door in the side panel *(right)*. This way, you won't have to unload the items at the front to remove a table from the back.

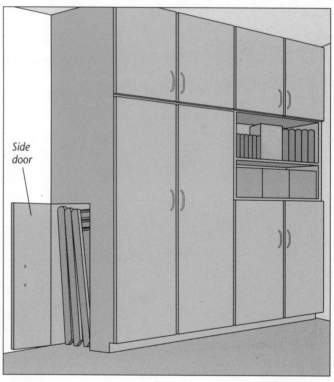

Side door

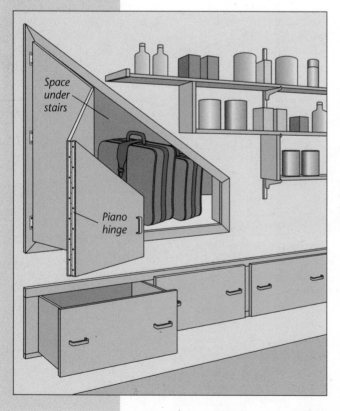

Space under stairs

Piano hinge

Under stairs
You can access the space under stairs—even if it's closed off by a wall. At the top of the space, cut a long, triangular hole for a door (being careful not to cut through any structural supports) and install a shelf below the opening. To avoid obstructions, make the door in three segments joined by piano hinges *(left)*. At the bottom of the space, install drawers. More ideas on storage under stairs are presented on page 8.

Building a customized garage unit

A sloping cabinet

The tapered shape of the storage unit shown below takes advantage of storage space in the upper part of a garage without encroaching on a car's clearance space. Start by cutting the vertical supports so they will span from the sole plate to the ceiling above when angled forward at 15°. Bolt the bottoms of the supports to the wall studs and the tops to the ceiling joists; you may need to add blocking between the framing members to anchor the supports if the spacing between the studs and joists is not suitable for your needs.

Next, saw shelf brackets from 2x4s, bolting the back ends to the studs. At the front, notch the back edges of the vertical supports to fit the brackets. Cut the shelves from 3/4" plywood and notch them to fit inside the studs at the back and the vertical supports at the front; the outside edges of the supports should extend 1" beyond the shelves. Cut the triangular side panels from 1/8" plywood and nail them to the studs and supports. Cover the exposed edges of the shelves with 1" thick trim nailed in place.

To complete the unit, cut the doors from 1/2" plywood, sizing them 1/8" shorter than their openings and 1/2" wider. The doors are not fixed in place; instead, they rest on the trim when closed and on 1x1 supports nailed to the shelf brackets when open.

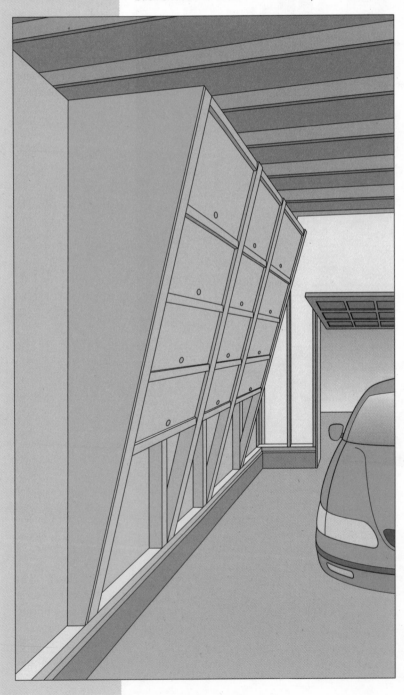

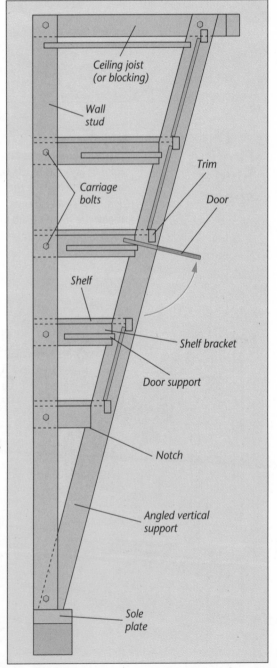

Ceiling joist (or blocking)

Wall stud

Carriage bolts

Trim

Door

Shelf

Shelf bracket

Door support

Notch

Angled vertical support

Sole plate

GARDENING TOOLS AND SUPPLIES

arden tools can be kept in a corner of a garage, but you may want to build a garage extension *(page 95)* or, if you don't have one already, a garden shed *(page 14)* to house a garden work center. You can set up a potting bench like the ones shown on the next page and, if you're ambitious, install a sink. Hang a chalkboard nearby for recording planting timetables and scheduling weekly gardening duties.

To store large equipment, such as lawn mowers and garden tillers, you'll need a spacious floor area with a clear path to the access door. Position the equipment so it doesn't block access to your potting bench. Make sure the door is wide enough for your biggest piece of machin-ery. If the door sills are high, you'll need to build ramps.

Organize light to medium-weight tools and supplies on a rack made of perforated hardboard *(page 43)*. Closed cabinets are best for garden poisons, sprayers, and extra-sharp tools—keep your cabinets locked to keep out children *(page 16)*. Seed packets and bottles can be stored on small shelves.

Fertilizers, potting soils, and chemicals should be sealed from moisture inside tight-closing cans or bins; metal containers help keep rodents and insects out of grass seed and bird feed.

To keep hoses untangled, you can buy a commercial hose reel or a rack like the one shown on page 26.

Finding hidden space

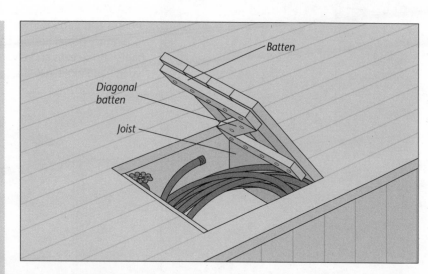

Batten

Diagonal batten

Joist

Reinforcing block

Under a deck

The space below the surface of most decks is ideal for storing garden tools or even a small barbecue. To install a trap door *(left, top)*, cut the decking so that the ends of the door rest on the center of a joist or beam. Build a compartment and attach it to the underside of the deck, drilling a hole in the bottom for drainage.

On the door's underside, fasten 1x3 battens offset from the ends and parallel to the joists or beams to keep the door securely seated. Add a third batten diagonally between the first two. Install a recessed pull on the door. You can simply set the door in place and lift it out as necessary, or use butt hinges to fasten one end to the deck.

Apply the same principles to install a door on a deck bench *(left, bottom)*, adding blocking to the underside of the seat to support the door's edge.

Building potting benches

Two garden centers

Either work center shown on this page will hold garden tools, pots, soil mixes and fertilizers efficiently. For either one, use exterior-grade plywood and apply a weatherproof finish if the cabinet will be located outside.

To build the fence- or wall-mounted cabinet (below, left), start by making the cabinet and shelf from ³/₄" plywood, reinforcing the top corners with 2x4 blocks. Attach the cabinet back to the fence, then assemble the work surface, using ³/₄" plywood for the benchtop. Use pressure-treated lumber for the 1x3 stretcher and 2x2 legs.

Fasten the legs to the work surface with butt hinges, adding the stretcher. Attach folding leg braces to lock the legs in place and strap hinges to fix the benchtop to the cabinet, and add a handle to the outside face of the top. To secure the bench in the folded-up position, attach swiveling cleats to blocks fastened to the cabinet top.

The freestanding work center (below, right) is basically a large cabinet with shelves, dividers, doors, and a fold-down work surface—all made from ³/₄" plywood. Use butt hinges to attach the work surface to the cabinet. Add a single leg with a butt hinge and folding leg braces.

Fasten hasps to the cabinet to hold the work surface in place when it is folded up. If you're storing soil or amendments inside the cabinet, you can drill ventilation holes into the sides.

CAUTION: Never cut pressure-treated wood indoors and don't burn it. Wear safety glasses and respiratory protection when cutting it, and long pants and sleeves and chemical-resistant gloves when handling it.

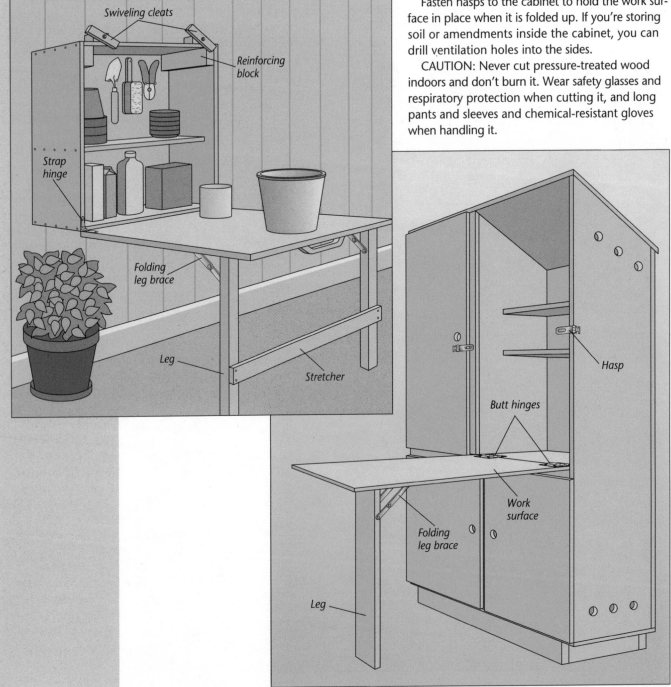

Storing soil mixtures

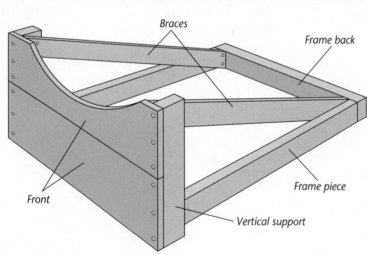

Braces

Frame back

Front

Frame piece

Vertical support

Garbage can racks

Metal garbage cans are ideal for storing peat moss, soil, and fertilizer. Build racks like these to hold the cans at an angle under a table.

Using pressure-treated lumber, cut the frame pieces and the vertical support from 2x4s and the diagonal braces from 1x3 stock. Make the front from 1-by lumber to suit the angle of the can.

CAUTION: Never cut pressure-treated wood indoors and don't burn it. Wear safety glasses and respiratory protection when cutting it, and long pants and sleeves and chemical-resistant gloves when handling it.

MAINTENANCE TIP

KEEPING TOOLS RUST-FREE

If you're putting your garden center to bed for the winter, tools need an environment where they won't rust; a dry area or closed cabinet is best. If rust-producing dampness is a problem, treat tools with liquid rust cleaner, emery paper, or a wire brush; then oil any working parts and apply a light coating of oil to surfaces that are susceptible to rust.

Storing garden equipment

Sliding door

Wood dowel

Carport closet

To store brooms, shovels, and other garden tools vertically, drill holes in two wood strips for dowels and glue in the dowels. Fasten the strips along a wall, as in the carport closet shown at left.

Prop the tool handles against the strip, between dowels, leaving valuable floor space for other supplies.

You may be able to build a closet in your carport that is deep enough to store a lawn mower, but make sure you leave sufficient clearance for your car (page 13).

STYLISH BARBECUE STORAGE

The most durable barbecue is set into a freestanding unit built from brick, stone, or concrete blocks. If you're designing a barbecue area, be sure to make room for storage.

Below the barbecue or to the side, you can build in cabinets for utensils, accessories, starter fluid, and charcoal briquettes; keep briquettes in metal or plastic cans with tight-fitting lids to keep out moisture. The well-lighted countertop and double-door cabinets shown below make barbecuing as convenient as cooking in the kitchen.

In addition to cabinets, barbecue storage can include shelves, hanging pegs, and drawers for tongs, oven mitts, and other small accessories.

Portable barbecues rust quickly when exposed to dampness and precipitation. A deep cabinet to house a portable barbecue can be built against the house wall, protected beneath the eaves.

TOOLS AND TECHNIQUES

To build your own storage units—simple wall systems, cabinets, and shelving—you'll need only basic carpentry skills, tools, and materials. In this chapter, we'll show you the tools and fasteners you're most likely to use. Then we'll introduce you to some of the simplest woodworking joints you can make to assemble your units. Finally, we'll give you an overview of the basic elements that make up the projects in this book: pegs and hooks, boxes and cases, shelves, doors, and drawers. With a little imagination, you can mix and match elements to meet your exact storage needs. If you don't want to start building from scratch, consider integrating some commercial products into your plans; some examples are given starting on page 20.

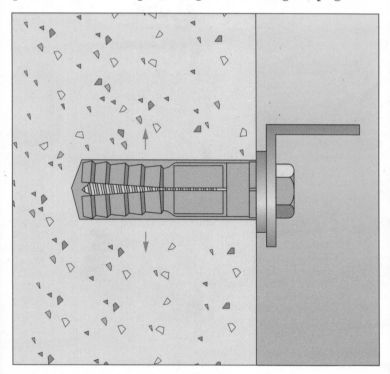

Techniques for fastening storage units to walls will depend on the kind of wall you're facing. Masonry walls in the garage or basement can pose a particular challenge. A lag screw anchored in an expansion shield as shown above provides a solid solution. In this chapter, we'll also show you how to fasten to wallboard or plaster walls, and how to locate studs.

TOOLS

Most of the projects in this book can be built using a few basic tools. These are illustrated below. In general, buy the best-quality tools you can afford—they'll pay for themselves in durability and performance.

When using a new power tool, read the owner's manual carefully and follow all safety directions. For more safety information on working with power tools, turn to page 17.

Always wear appropriate safety equipment, including the following:

• Safety goggles or glasses when operating power tools or when using a striking tool, especially when fastening into concrete.

• Gloves: Wear work gloves when handling wood, and rubber or plastic gloves when working with harmful substances such as solvents or wood preservatives.

• A respirator when using substances such as adhesives and paints that give off toxic fumes.

• A dust mask when creating sawdust, such as when sawing or sanding.

• Earmuff protectors or earplugs if you're using power tools for extended periods.

TOOLS OF THE TRADE

Circular saw
Equipped with a combination blade, handles cuts both along and across the grain; 7¼" model is most common.

Saber saw
Ideal for curves and interior cuts; can also be used for straight cuts.

Bench chisel
For paring waste from dadoes and rabbets; can be used with hand pressure alone or tapped with a mallet.

Electric drill
Variable-speed models can be used for power screwdriving as well as drilling. Choose a ³/₈" model that is reversible and double-insulated. Cordless models are very handy.

Carpenter's level
For checking both level and plumb. A longer level gives a more accurate reading.

Pipe clamp
For gluing up large boxes, cases, and panels. Jaws attach to steel pipe; length can be adjusted as needed.

Combination square
For marking or checking 90° and 45° angles. Also for gauging depth when cutting dadoes.

Jack plane
Squares and smoothes edges and faces of boards; use block plane for end grain.

Router
Used to cut dadoes and rabbets, or shape the edges of wood.

Hacksaw
Cuts metals and plastic; blade can be attached with cutting edge up or down.

C-clamp
Standard clamp for small jobs, such as securing straightedge guides to stock; common jaw openings are 4", 6", and 8".

Adjustable wrench
For gripping nuts, bolts, and lag screws; choose a 10" model for general-purpose use. Open-end wrenches and box wrenches fit nuts and bolts more precisely, but you'll need a whole set; box wrenches allow you to apply more pressure.

Claw hammer
For driving nails; choose model with a 16-ounce head. Use with a nailset for driving nails flush without marring wood.

Tape measure
Available in lengths from 8' to 25'; locking button prevents tape from retracting.

FASTENERS

To assemble storage units, you'll need glue, nails, screws, and bolts. Some of the most commonly used fasteners are illustrated below. In most cases, adhesives won't be strong enough alone, but you can use them in combination with nails or screws. Nails are easy to use, but screws provide more strength. To hide nails, set them with a nailset and cover them with wood putty.

Bolts are the strongest of all; they pass completely through a material and are tightened down with a nut threaded onto the end. Most bolts require a washer at each side of the nut to either distribute the load or keep the nut from loosening. Another alternative is knock-down hardware—fasteners that enable you to take an assembly apart for transportation or storage.

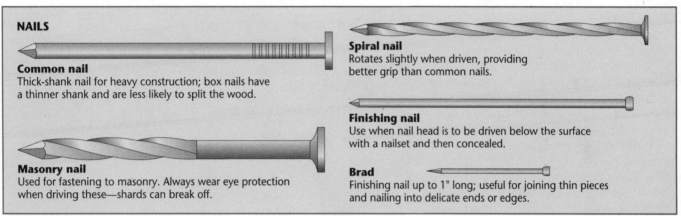

NAILS

Common nail
Thick-shank nail for heavy construction; box nails have a thinner shank and are less likely to split the wood.

Masonry nail
Used for fastening to masonry. Always wear eye protection when driving these—shards can break off.

Spiral nail
Rotates slightly when driven, providing better grip than common nails.

Finishing nail
Use when nail head is to be driven below the surface with a nailset and then concealed.

Brad
Finishing nail up to 1" long; useful for joining thin pieces and nailing into delicate ends or edges.

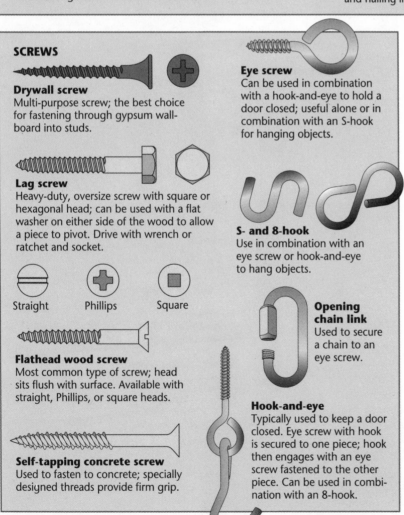

SCREWS

Drywall screw
Multi-purpose screw; the best choice for fastening through gypsum wallboard into studs.

Lag screw
Heavy-duty, oversize screw with square or hexagonal head; can be used with a flat washer on either side of the wood to allow a piece to pivot. Drive with wrench or ratchet and socket.

Straight   Phillips   Square

Flathead wood screw
Most common type of screw; head sits flush with surface. Available with straight, Phillips, or square heads.

Self-tapping concrete screw
Used to fasten to concrete; specially designed threads provide firm grip.

Eye screw
Can be used in combination with a hook-and-eye to hold a door closed; useful alone or in combination with an S-hook for hanging objects.

S- and 8-hook
Use in combination with an eye screw or hook-and-eye to hang objects.

Opening chain link
Used to secure a chain to an eye screw.

Hook-and-eye
Typically used to keep a door closed. Eye screw with hook is secured to one piece; hook then engages with an eye screw fastened to the other piece. Can be used in combination with an 8-hook.

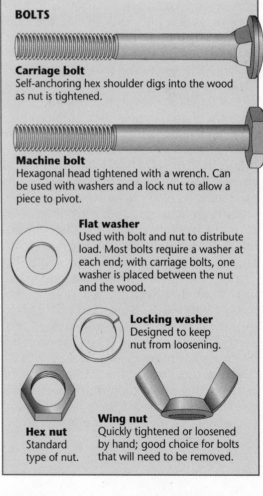

BOLTS

Carriage bolt
Self-anchoring hex shoulder digs into the wood as nut is tightened.

Machine bolt
Hexagonal head tightened with a wrench. Can be used with washers and a lock nut to allow a piece to pivot.

Flat washer
Used with bolt and nut to distribute load. Most bolts require a washer at each end; with carriage bolts, one washer is placed between the nut and the wood.

Locking washer
Designed to keep nut from loosening.

Hex nut
Standard type of nut.

Wing nut
Quickly tightened or loosened by hand; good choice for bolts that will need to be removed.

BASIC JOINERY

Boxes, frames, and shelves are the building blocks of do-it-yourself storage units. Whether you're assembling a large cabinet or a simple rack, you'll need to join pieces of wood. In this section, we'll show you how to make three basic joints—butt, lap, and dado. Simple to make, these joints will be adequate for most of the storage units you'll want to make for your base-

ment, attic, and garage. Each joint has specific uses. Butt joints are your simplest choice for assembling frames and boxes or making wide boards from narrow stock. Lap joints are useful in situations where two boards cross, as in the bicycle rack shown on page 58. Dado joints are an attractive and sturdy method for fixing shelves to the inside of a cabinet.

BUTT JOINTS

Whether you're joining the corners of a box or frame, or gluing several narrow boards together edge to edge to form a shelf or panel, most of the projects in this book call for attaching the face or edge of one board to the face, edge, or end of another. The easiest joinery method for these situations is a butt joint—the two pieces simply butt up against each other.

Depending on how the boards are being connected, some butt joints need only be glued together. When the two pieces are being joined along their length as in the edge-to-edge or edge-to-face joints shown at right, glue is sufficient; in fact, the glue bond along the joint lines will be stronger than the wood fibers holding the boards together. The pieces will have to be clamped while the glue dries.

Any butt joint involving end grain, on the other hand, cannot rely on glue and clamping alone. Additional reinforcement is necessary. The end-to-face joint, commonly used to build boxes and cases, can be strengthened in a number of ways. The simplest method is to use nails or screws; the latter make for a stronger joint. In general, choose a nail or screw that is three times longer than the thickness of the first piece you are driving the fastener into.

Glue blocks, through dowels, and wood biscuits offer more attractive ways of reinforcing butt joints. Glue blocks are glued into the corners of a case and secured in place with small brads. If you use dowels, buy fluted or spiral-groove dowels with a diameter equal to half the thickness of your stock. To make plate (or biscuit) joints, you'll need a plate joiner. But these joints are easy to cut and provide excellent reinforcement.

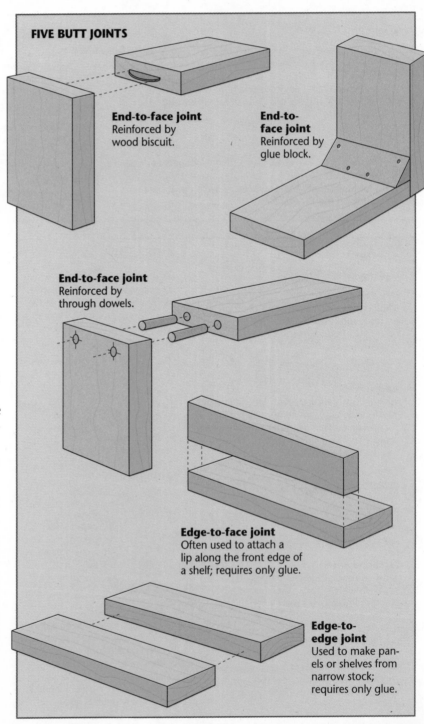

FIVE BUTT JOINTS

End-to-face joint
Reinforced by wood biscuit.

End-to-face joint
Reinforced by glue block.

End-to-face joint
Reinforced by through dowels.

Edge-to-face joint
Often used to attach a lip along the front edge of a shelf; requires only glue.

Edge-to-edge joint
Used to make panels or shelves from narrow stock; requires only glue.

Reinforcing corners with through dowels

1. Preparing the stock

When making an end-to-face joint, be sure to cut the pieces so their ends and edges are perfectly square to each other. Cut the boards on a table saw or radial-arm saw.

You can use a circular saw instead, but you'll need a straightedge to guide the cut. If your stock is narrow enough, you can cut the wood with a backsaw and miter box.

2. Reinforcing with through dowels

Glue and clamp the joint. Then, once the glue has cured, remove the clamps and drill holes through the face of one piece and 3/4" into the adjoining piece. Bore two holes per joint. Cut the dowels slightly longer than the depth of the holes. Coat the dowels sparingly with glue and tap them into the holes with a mallet *(right)*.

Once the glue has cured, saw off the excess dowel and sand the surface flush.

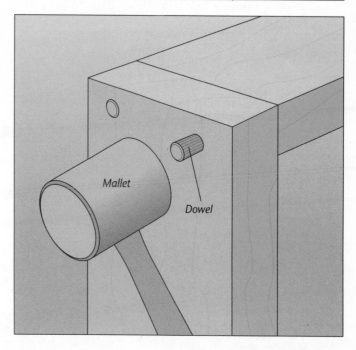

Mallet

Dowel

Making a panel from boards

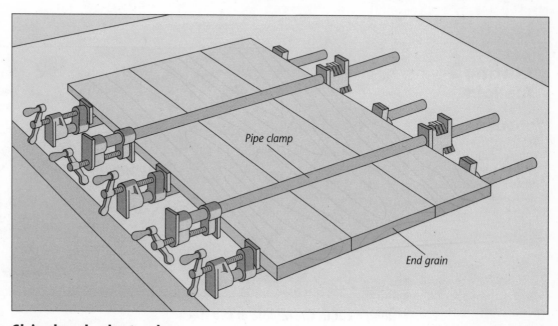

Pipe clamp

End grain

Gluing boards edge to edge

If you have a large stock of straight boards on hand, you can use them to make wide shelves or panels for a case by simply gluing them together.

Start by truing the edges of the stock with a jointer or hand plane. Then spread an even coat of white glue on the board's contacting edges and secure them together using pipe or bar clamps. Use as many clamps as necessary to support the boards at 12" to 18" intervals, alternating the clamps between the top and bottom of the stock *(above)*.

Tighten the clamps a little at a time until there are no gaps between the boards and adhesive squeezes out of all the joints. To minimize warping, alternate the end grain direction of adjacent boards, as shown.

LAP JOINTS

Lap joints are used to join two pieces of wood that overlap. They are formed by cutting recesses across the grain of one or both pieces of wood. These recesses are referred to as dadoes (*opposite*) when they're in the middle of the piece of wood, and as rabbets when they're at the end.

Lap joints are glued and clamped together, but end and T half-lap joints may also need to be reinforced with nails, screws, or dowels. Cross half laps usually don't need to be reinforced, as the extra shoulder helps lock the pieces together.

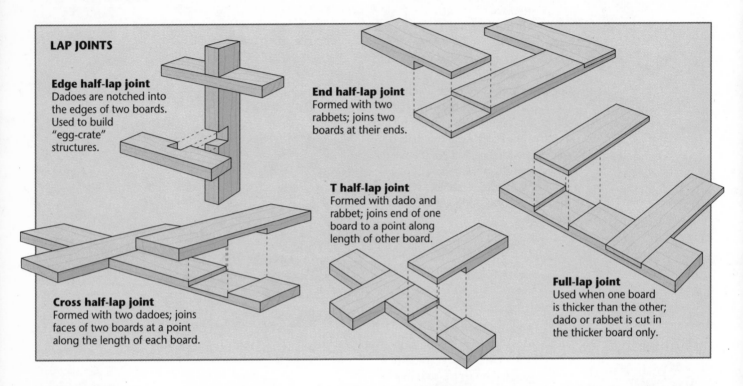

LAP JOINTS

Edge half-lap joint
Dadoes are notched into the edges of two boards. Used to build "egg-crate" structures.

End half-lap joint
Formed with two rabbets; joins two boards at their ends.

T half-lap joint
Formed with dado and rabbet; joins end of one board to a point along length of other board.

Cross half-lap joint
Formed with two dadoes; joins faces of two boards at a point along the length of each board.

Full-lap joint
Used when one board is thicker than the other; dado or rabbet is cut in the thicker board only.

Cutting a lap joint

TOOLKIT
• Clamps
• Router with straight bit
• Bench chisel and mallet
• Block plane (optional)

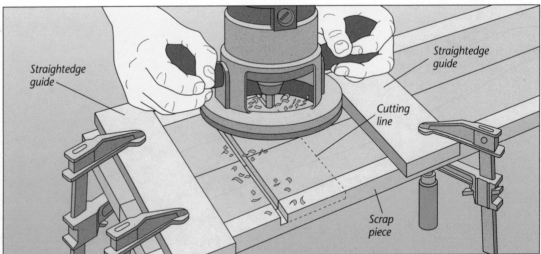

Straightedge guide

Straightedge guide

Cutting line

Scrap piece

Making a cut in the middle of the stock

To cut a wide dado, mark both edges of the recess. Clamp the stock to your workbench, adding a scrap piece along each edge to prevent the edges from splintering. (For a cross half-lap joint, you can cut both pieces at once, provided they're exactly the same width.)

Adjust the router so the depth of cut is exactly half the stock's thickness. Set two straightedges by measuring the distance from the edge of the bit to the edge of the base plate and clamping the straightedge at this distance from your cutting lines. Next, make two cuts just to the waste side of the cutting lines to define the outline of the dado; keep the router's base plate against the guides. Finally, remove the remaining waste with passes down the middle, and then smooth with a chisel if necessary.

Making a cut at the end of the stock
To make a wide rabbet cut, clamp your work in the same way as for the wide dado *(opposite)*, except use only one straightedge.

Measure from the edge of the bit to the edge of the base plate of your router and clamp the straightedge at this distance from your cutting line. Remove most of the waste by moving in with the router from the end of the stock toward the cutting line, always cutting against the rotation of the router bit. Then make a final pass, using the straightedge as a guide. Finally, smooth the rabbet with a chisel or block plane.

DADO JOINTS

A dado joint is made by cutting a groove across one face of a board. Dadoes are often used to join a shelf or vertical partition to the inside of a case. They can also be used to join the sides of a box to the bottom.

The first step in making a dado is to measure and mark the outside edges. Then set a combination square for the depth of the recess and mark the bottom of the cut. The cut should be one quarter to one third the thickness of the board. To make the cuts, you can use a circular saw, as shown below, or a router, as shown opposite.

If you're cutting dadoes to attach shelves to a case, clamp the two sides of the case together and make the cuts in both at once so that they will line up.

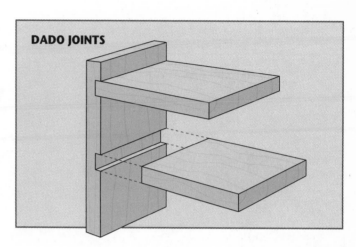

DADO JOINTS

Making a dado joint

TOOLKIT
• Clamps
• Circular saw
• Bench chisel and mallet
• Jack plane or sanding block (optional)

1 **Making the cuts**
Measure from the outside edges of the circular saw blade to each side of the base plate and mark these two points on the stock on each side of the recess you want to cut. Clamp the guide to one of the marks—the saw blade should be on the waste side of one cutting line.

Cut the length of the recess, holding the base plate tight against the guide. Relocate the guide and cut the other side *(right)*; then, make several cuts between the first two.

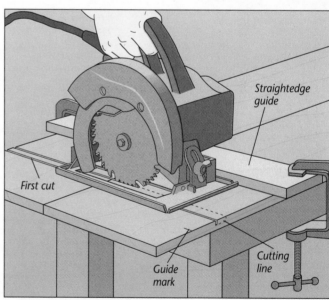

Straightedge guide

First cut

Guide mark

Cutting line

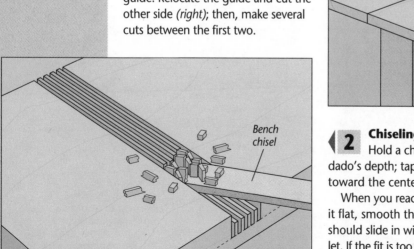

Bench chisel

2 **Chiseling out the waste**
Hold a chisel, bevel side down, at a point about half the dado's depth; tap it lightly with a mallet to remove waste. Work toward the center, gradually lowering the depth of your cuts.

When you reach the bottom, turn the chisel over and, holding it flat, smooth the dado. Check the fit of the second board; it should slide in with light hand pressure or a few taps with a mallet. If the fit is too tight, plane or sand the second board rather than making the dado wider.

PEGS AND HOOKS

Hanging objects from walls and ceilings frees up valuable space on your floors and worktables. A wide variety of special hardware is available, a selection of which is illustrated below.

You can buy simple hooks for hanging virtually anything or use specialized hardware designed for holding specific items such as bicycles or mops. A perforated hardboard (Peg-Board) rack with hooks is one of the most versatile ways of holding tools and other small objects.

Although some hardware can be applied with self-stick adhesive, most of the projects in this book require pegs and hooks to be attached more securely— using nails or screws. For maximum holding power, always fasten into a material that your nail or screw can get a good grip on, like wall studs, ceiling joists, or a masonry wall. If you can't locate the studs or joists, you can hang lightweight items from plaster or wallboard using one of the special fasteners featured on 80.

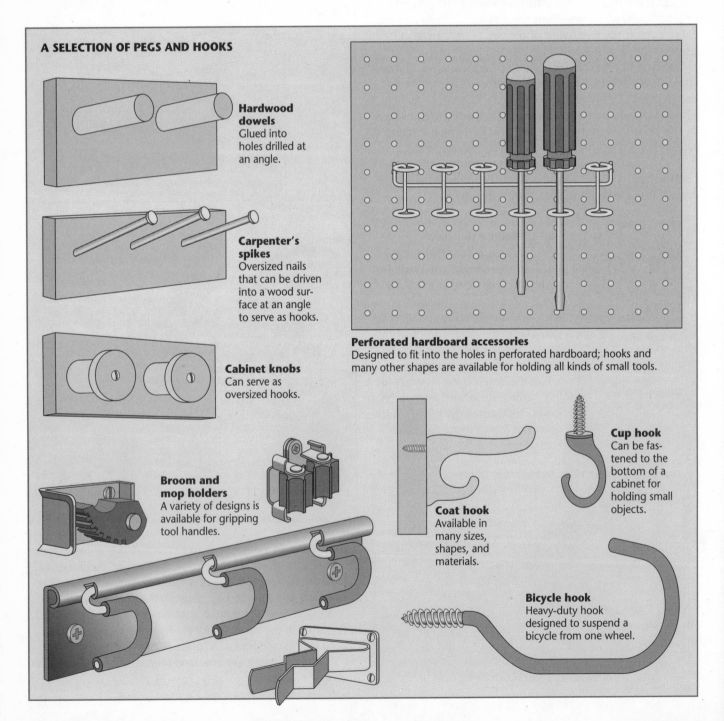

A SELECTION OF PEGS AND HOOKS

Hardwood dowels
Glued into holes drilled at an angle.

Carpenter's spikes
Oversized nails that can be driven into a wood surface at an angle to serve as hooks.

Cabinet knobs
Can serve as oversized hooks.

Perforated hardboard accessories
Designed to fit into the holes in perforated hardboard; hooks and many other shapes are available for holding all kinds of small tools.

Broom and mop holders
A variety of designs is available for gripping tool handles.

Coat hook
Available in many sizes, shapes, and materials.

Cup hook
Can be fastened to the bottom of a cabinet for holding small objects.

Bicycle hook
Heavy-duty hook designed to suspend a bicycle from one wheel.

Drilling at an angle for dowels

TOOLKIT
• Electric drill
• Adjustable T-bevel or commercial drill guide

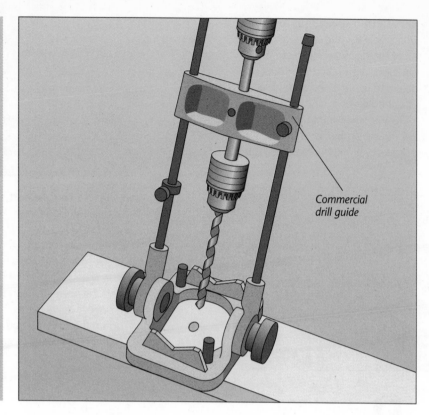

Commercial drill guide

Keeping the bit at the right angle

Install a brad-point bit or, for larger holes, a spade bit in your drill. You can use an adjustable T-bevel as a guide to keep the tool at the right angle. Set it up next to where you want to drill the hole and follow the angle of the blade by eye.

For more accuracy, use a commercial drill guide like the one shown at left. Adjust the guide to the appropriate angle —you can also use the guide to set the drilling depth—and bore the hole. Squirt some glue in the hole and insert the dowel.

Fastening to wall studs and ceiling joists

TOOLKIT
• Stud finder (optional)
• Screwdriver or electric drill

Locating and attaching to studs and joists

When hanging anything heavy from a ceiling or stud wall, fasten to studs or joists. These framing members are usually spaced 16" or 24" apart on center (from center to center), as shown below. The trick is locating the first one. Try knocking on the wall with the heel of your hand. A solid sound indicates a stud; a hollow sound is the space between.

You can also look for the fasteners in your wallboard or paneling; they probably correspond to the location of a stud. If you can't see the fasteners, use a stud finder *(inset)*. With the type shown, the red light indicates when the device reaches a stud or joist. If all else fails, drill small exploratory holes in the wall or ceiling.

Once you've found the studs or joists, use drywall screws to attach a storage unit to a wall or the ceiling. These can be power-driven into the stud or joist without drilling a pilot hole.

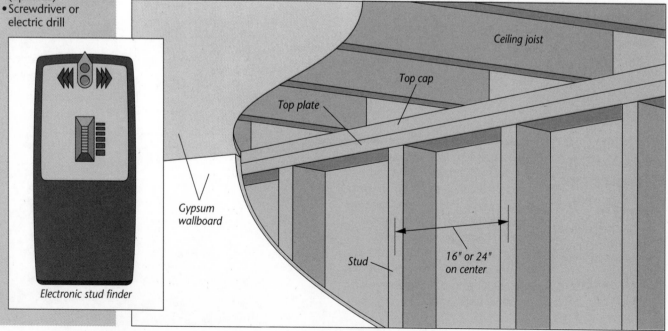

Electronic stud finder

Gypsum wallboard

Top plate

Top cap

Ceiling joist

Stud

16" or 24" on center

Fastening to wallboard or plaster

TOOLKIT
• Electric drill
• Screwdriver

Installing a spreading anchor
Drill a hole through the wall, using a bit of the diameter indicated on the package. Slip the screw through the object to be attached and thread it into the sleeve.

Push the sleeve into the wall and tighten the screw; as shown at right, the sleeve will expand against the back of the wall.

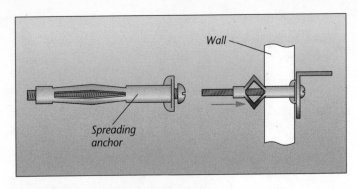

Wall

Spreading anchor

Installing a toggle bolt
Drill a hole through the wall large enough to fit the screw and toggle when it is retracted. Slip the screw through the object to be attached and thread on the toggle; make sure the screw is long enough to go all the way through the wall. Then pass the fastener through the hole—the spring-loaded toggle will open once it clears the wall.

Tug on the screw as you begin tightening it; this will pull the toggle up against the back side of the wall *(left)*.

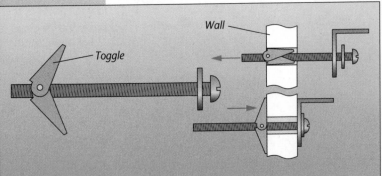

Wall

Toggle

 ASK A PRO

HOW DO I INSTALL PERFORATED HARDBOARD (PEG-BOARD)?
The trick with perforated hardboard is to install it with a space behind it so the pegs or hooks can fit through. To do this, slip a spacer over the screw before threading it into the anchor or toggle. The spacer will hold the board out from the wall, as shown at right.

Alternatively, you can fasten furring strips to the wall behind the board, and attach the board to these strips.

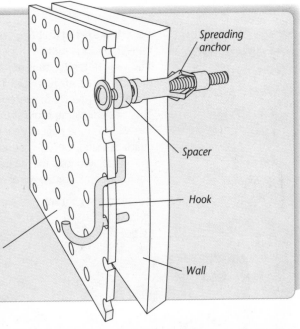

Spreading anchor

Spacer

Hook

Wall

Perforated hardboard

Fastening to masonry

TOOLKIT
• Electric drill with masonry bit
• Ball-peen hammer
• Adjustable wrench or open-end wrench

Installing an expansion shield
Drill a hole into the wall equal to the the sleeve diameter—and slightly longer—then tap the sleeve in using a ball-peen hammer. Slip a lag screw through the item to be hung and tighten it into the sleeve *(right)*.

To fasten furring strips or light-weight brackets to masonry, you can use self-tapping concrete screws or masonry nails *(page 73)*.

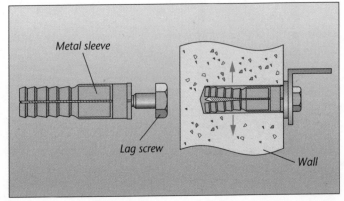

Metal sleeve

Lag screw

Wall

BOXES, BINS, AND CASES

Boxes, bins, and cases are all built in essentially the same way. They consist of five basic pieces—two sides, a back, and a top and bottom; shelves are optional. The easiest way to join the pieces of a box is with butt joints, as discussed on page 74. If the top will have to bear weight, cut it to overlap the sides so that it is adequately supported. If a box is to be lifted while it is loaded, attach the bottom to the inside of the sides so it doesn't pull off when the box is lifted off the floor. If you want a kick space below a box or case, attach the bottom to the sides with dadoes, as shown at right.

To assemble the box, first put glue in the dadoes and attach the two sides to the base, reinforcing the joints. Then, attach the top. Finally, attach the back—first fasten one edge, then square the box and fasten the other edge.

In the case shown at right, the top is joined to the sides with rabbet joints. (You can also use butt joints, as for the box.) For lightweight storage, you can attach the shelves with reinforced butt joints *(page 74)*, but you'll get a sturdier unit using dado joints. Cut the dadoes in both sides at the same time so they line up. The best tool to use for both dadoes and rabbets is the router *(page 76)*, unless you have a table saw or a radial-arm saw equipped with a dado blade. But as shown on page 77, you can cut a dado with a circular saw.

To assemble the case, spread glue in the rabbets and dadoes, then lay one side piece on a worktable. Slip the top and shelves in place and fit the other side on top. Secure the assembly with pipe or bar clamps, using two clamps for each joint. Reinforce the joints with nails or screws.

You can also attach shelves with ledgers *(page 83)*. For adjustable shelves, install tracks with clips *(page 83)* or drill two vertical rows of dowel holes on the inside faces of the sides; the shelves rest on dowels which can be moved around as necessary. Adding a door to a case *(page 86)* transforms it into a cabinet.

In general, build cases using 1-by lumber or $^3/_4$-inch plywood; $^1/_2$-inch plywood or hardboard is adequate for backs.

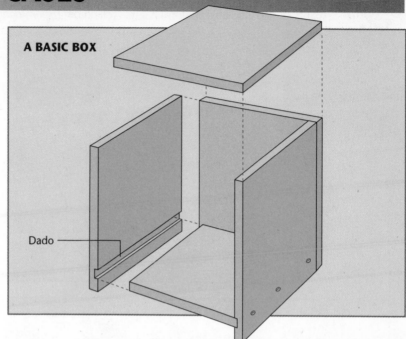

A BASIC BOX

Dado

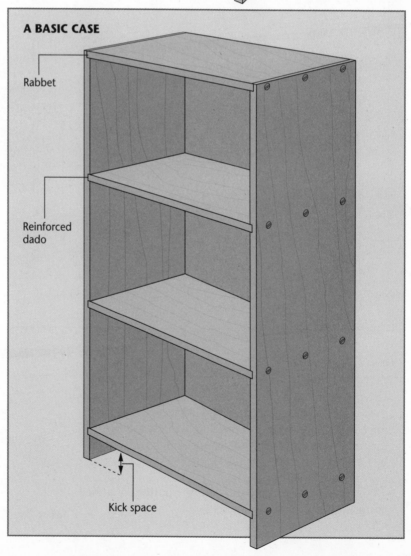

A BASIC CASE

Rabbet

Reinforced dado

Kick space

Adapting the basic box

Tilting and rolling bins

Attach a box to a counter with hinges to create a tilt-out bin *(below, left)* that provides access to areas under the counter or at the bottom of a cabinet or closet. Fasten casters to a box to transform it into a rolling bin *(below, right)* that can be moved around.

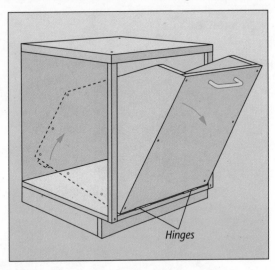

Hinges

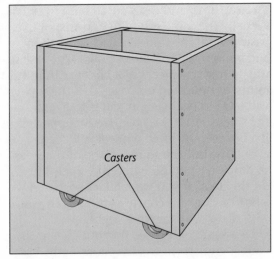

Casters

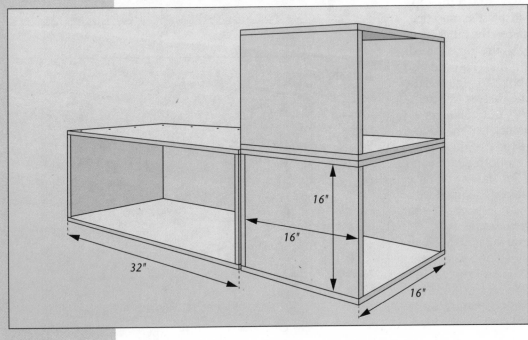

16"

16"

16"

32"

Modular boxes

To build a set of stacking bins, make several boxes of the same size, or rectangular units that are twice as long as square ones, as shown at left. High stacks of boxes should be bolted together or bolted to the wall.

READY ROD ATTACHMENTS

To install a rod inside a cabinet or closet, use pole sockets *(near right)*. First, screw one socket in place, then insert the rod and level it before fastening the other socket. If the rod is very long, you can provide additional support by fastening a hook to the top or back of the case near the middle of the rod.

You can also suspend a rod from the bottom of a shelf using closet rod brackets *(far right)*.

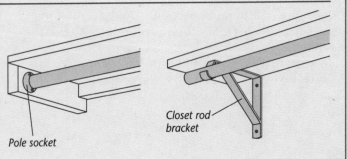

Pole socket

Closet rod bracket

SHELVES

Sturdy shelves can be made from a number of different materials: solid lumber—pine, fir, and other softwoods—or plywood or particleboard. Plywood and particleboard are less expensive than solid wood, but not as strong. Plywood is stronger than particleboard. Plywood and particleboard are both available covered with melamine or laminate, which makes the shelving more attractive and relatively easy to maintain; laminate is more durable than melamine. For deep shelving, use plywood or solid-wood shelves made from boards edge-glued together *(page 75)*.

A variety of brackets is available for attaching shelves to walls, including shelf brackets, L-braces, track-and-

bracket systems, and Z-brackets *(below)*. To support heavy objects, the brackets should be fastened into a stud or a masonry wall; for lightweight storage, you can fasten to wallboard or plaster *(page 80)*.

If the studs are exposed, you can use special brackets that fit around studs or attach ledgers to the sides of the studs to support shallow shelving. To fix shelves to the inside of a case *(page 81)*, use dadoes. You can also attach brackets or braces to the back or sides of the case; tracks and clips to the sides; or ledgers to the sides and back; or drill holes in the sides for supporting dowels. For lightweight storage, you can fasten shelves with reinforced butt joints *(page 74)*.

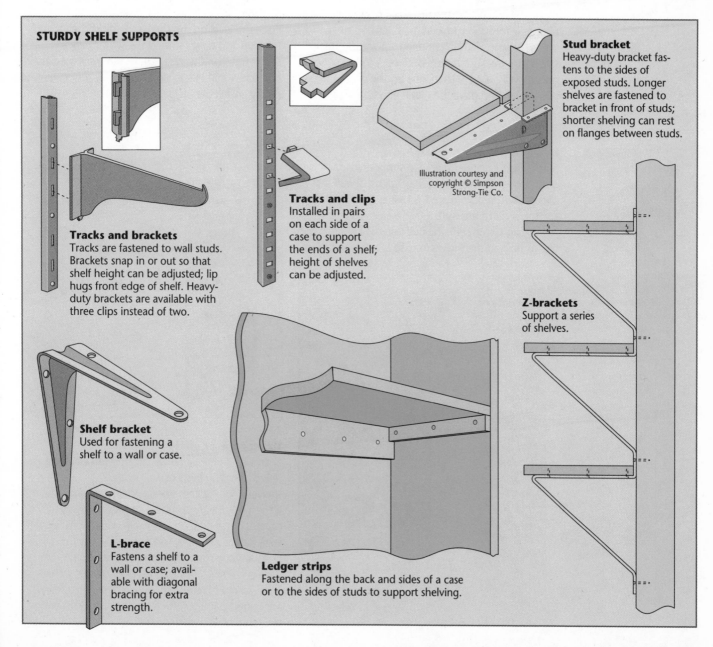

STURDY SHELF SUPPORTS

Tracks and brackets
Tracks are fastened to wall studs. Brackets snap in or out so that shelf height can be adjusted; lip hugs front edge of shelf. Heavy-duty brackets are available with three clips instead of two.

Tracks and clips
Installed in pairs on each side of a case to support the ends of a shelf; height of shelves can be adjusted.

Stud bracket
Heavy-duty bracket fastens to the sides of exposed studs. Longer shelves are fastened to bracket in front of studs; shorter shelving can rest on flanges between studs.

Illustration courtesy and copyright © Simpson Strong-Tie Co.

Z-brackets
Support a series of shelves.

Shelf bracket
Used for fastening a shelf to a wall or case.

L-brace
Fastens a shelf to a wall or case; available with diagonal bracing for extra strength.

Ledger strips
Fastened along the back and sides of a case or to the sides of studs to support shelving.

Mounting tracks and brackets

TOOLKIT
- Hacksaw
- Stud finder (optional)
- Electric drill
- Screwdriver
- Carpenter's level

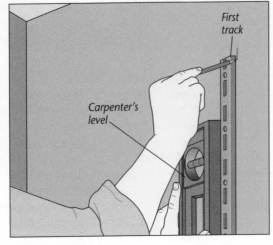

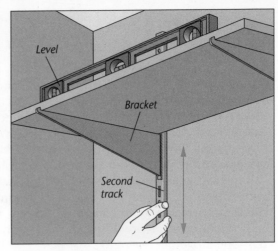

1 Installing the first track

Cut the tracks to length with a hacksaw, making sure the slots will align. Locate the wall studs *(page 79)* and center the first track over one. Drill a pilot hole through a hole in the track and drive in a screw, leaving it loose enough to pivot the track. Check the track for plumb and mark a line along it on the wall *(above)*. Then, line up the track, bore pilot holes, and drive the remaining screws.

2 Installing the second track and the shelf

Insert a bracket in the first track and one in the matching slot of the second track. Holding the second track in position, lay a shelf across the brackets. Place the level on the shelf and adjust the second track up and down to level the shelf. Mark the top of the track on the wall. Check the track for plumb and screw it in place, aligning it with the mark. Finally, install the brackets and the shelf.

Building shelving systems

TOOLKIT
For a rope or chain system:
- Electric drill
- Adjustable wrench
- Screwdriver for electrical cable clamps (optional)

Using bricks and boards

Stack bricks or cinder blocks to support solid lumber or plywood shelves, preferably against a wall, as shown at right. If your stack is higher than 5', anchor the top shelf to the wall.

You can create cubbyholes if you use chimney flue tiles to support the shelves instead of bricks or blocks.

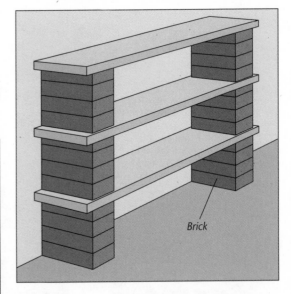

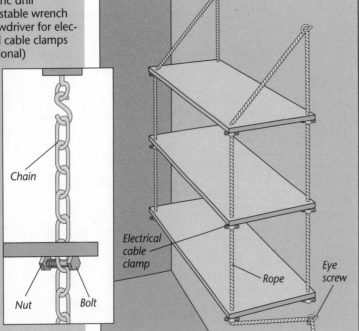

Using rope or chain

Shelving can be suspended from ropes or chains fastened to ceiling joists or wall studs. Drill holes in the shelves and pass the ropes or chains through them. If you use rope, support the shelves by knotting the rope or installing electrical cable clamps below each shelf *(left)*. For chains, use nuts and bolts *(inset)*.

Attach the ropes or chains to the wall or joists with eye screws, using S-hooks or opening chain links *(page 73)* to join the chain to the eye screw. For added stability, also anchor the bottom end of the ropes or chains to the wall.

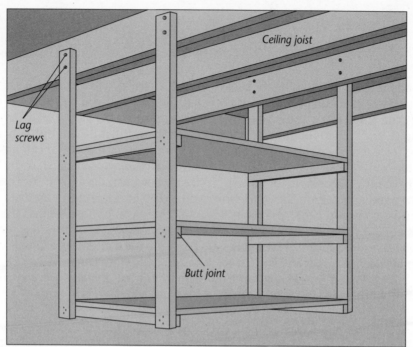

Ceiling joist

Lag screws

Butt joint

Using ladder supports

Build ladder supports from 2x4 or larger lumber. For lightweight storage, fasten the pieces together with standard wood screws; for heavier storage, use lag screws or bolts. You can also use lap joints *(page 76)*.

Fasten the supports to the ceiling joists with lag screws or bolts; for a freestanding unit, tie the parts together with cross braces. In either case, nail the shelves in place to stabilize the unit.

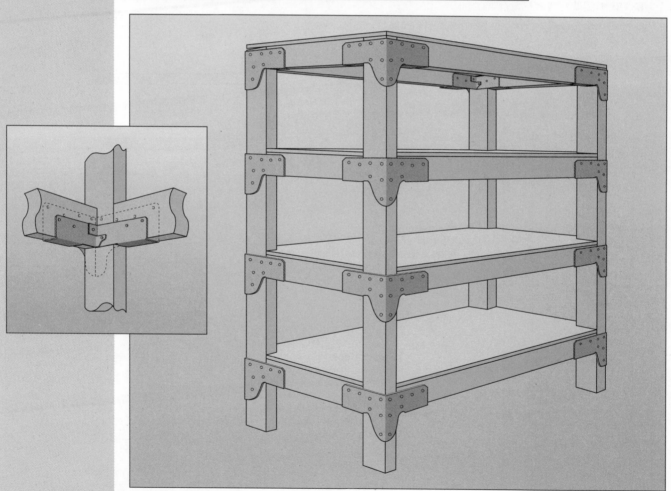

Illustrations courtesy and copyright © Simpson Strong-Tie Co.

Using metal connectors

Commercial metal connectors like those shown above can be used to quickly assemble heavy-duty shelving units. Screw the connectors to the vertical and horizontal pieces to hold them all together *(inset)*.

DOORS

When you've finished building your cabinet or closet, you're ready to attach the doors. For most units, you can choose among the three types shown below: hinged, sliding, or bifold doors. Roll-ups of plastic or canvas are an economical choice, but they're not as durable or protective as other doors.

There is a wide variety of hinges available for attaching doors; some of most popular types are shown opposite. Butt hinges, the most common type, are usually installed on the inside edges of the door and frame; unless you set the hinge leaves into mortises, you will have to leave a wide gap between the door and the frame. To hang a hinged door, first fasten one leaf of each hinge to the door. Then hold the door in position and mark the top screw holes in the free leaves on the cabinet. Install the top screws, check the swing and alignment of the door, and if you are satisfied with everything, install the bottom screws.

Some common types of catches are also shown opposite. For overlay doors, fasten the catch to the cabinet frame; for flush doors, mount them on fixed shelves—at the top or bottom. If you live in an earthquake area, make sure you choose a catch that won't shake loose; for information on earthquake security, turn to page 17. To secure the contents of a closet or cabinet from children, install childproof catches (page 16). To keep the contents safe from theft, install a security hasp like the one shown on page 18.

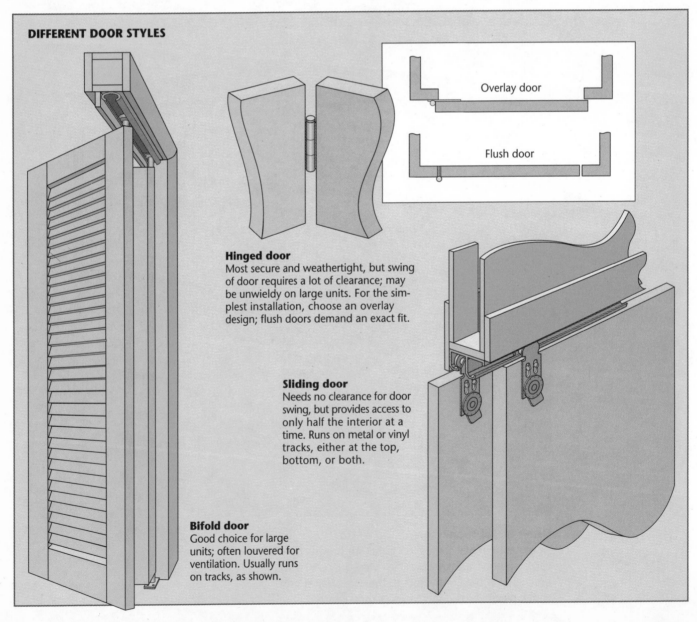

DIFFERENT DOOR STYLES

Overlay door

Flush door

Hinged door
Most secure and weathertight, but swing of door requires a lot of clearance; may be unwieldy on large units. For the simplest installation, choose an overlay design; flush doors demand an exact fit.

Sliding door
Needs no clearance for door swing, but provides access to only half the interior at a time. Runs on metal or vinyl tracks, either at the top, bottom, or both.

Bifold door
Good choice for large units; often louvered for ventilation. Usually runs on tracks, as shown.

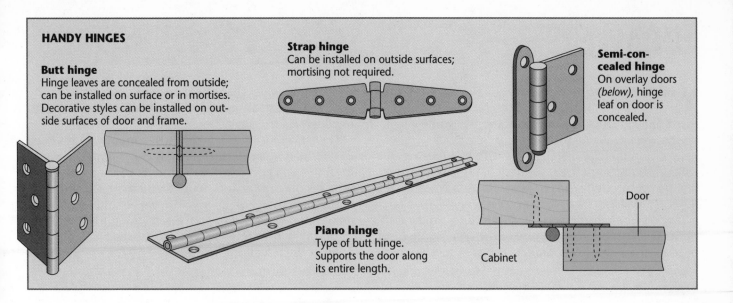

HANDY HINGES

Butt hinge
Hinge leaves are concealed from outside; can be installed on surface or in mortises. Decorative styles can be installed on outside surfaces of door and frame.

Strap hinge
Can be installed on outside surfaces; mortising not required.

Semi-concealed hinge
On overlay doors *(below)*, hinge leaf on door is concealed.

Piano hinge
Type of butt hinge. Supports the door along its entire length.

Door

Cabinet

Chiseling out a hinge mortise

TOOLKIT
- Sharp knife
- Bench chisel
- Mallet

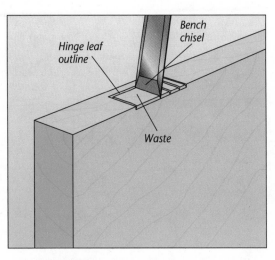

Hinge leaf outline

Bench chisel

Waste

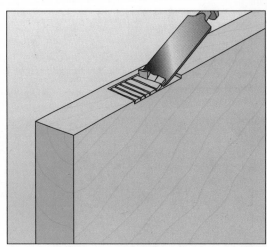

1 Scoring the hinge outline
Outline the hinge leaf on the surface, then score your marks using a sharp knife. Holding a bench chisel vertically—bevel facing the waste—tap it lightly with a mallet to deepen the scored lines to the full depth of the mortise; use a chisel of the same width as the mortise. Then make a series of cross-grain cuts every 1/4" from one end of the outline to the other *(above)*.

2 Chiseling out the waste
With the bevel facing down and flat on the surface, chip out the waste wood using hand pressure alone *(above)*. (For a mortise that goes right to the edge, as shown, you can also hold the chisel horizontally and cut the waste away by keeping the flat side of the blade against the bottom of the mortise.) Clean up the mortise holding the chisel flat, bevel up, and working across the grain.

COMMON CATCHES

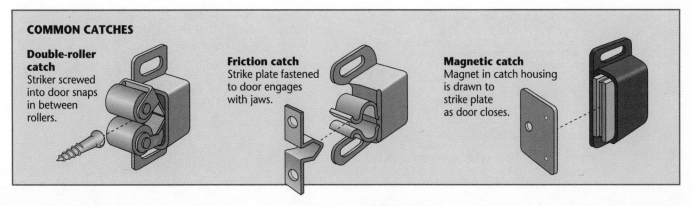

Double-roller catch
Striker screwed into door snaps in between rollers.

Friction catch
Strike plate fastened to door engages with jaws.

Magnetic catch
Magnet in catch housing is drawn to strike plate as door closes.

DRAWERS

You can build your own drawers—a tricky job for the beginner—or choose from a selection of manufactured drawers. Installation hardware may come with the drawers or you can choose from the guides shown below. Commercial metal guides with ball-bearings or rollers usually work the smoothest. Simpler systems relying on wooden strips or plastic channels work well for most loads.

If you've bought drawers, you'll need to build a frame to fit. This can be a simple case of the type featured on page 81. The opening should be about 1/4 inch higher

and 1/8 inch wider than the drawer. If you're installing commercial side-mounted guides, you'll generally need to allow 1/2 inch on each side.

The guides and runners on most commercial systems have one or more elongated screw holes that provide for fine-tuning during installation. Position the hardware on the drawer and cabinet, and mark the center of the elongated holes. Drive the screws and test-fit the drawer. If necessary, loosen the screws slightly and reposition the hardware. Once you are satisfied with the fit, drive in the remaining screws.

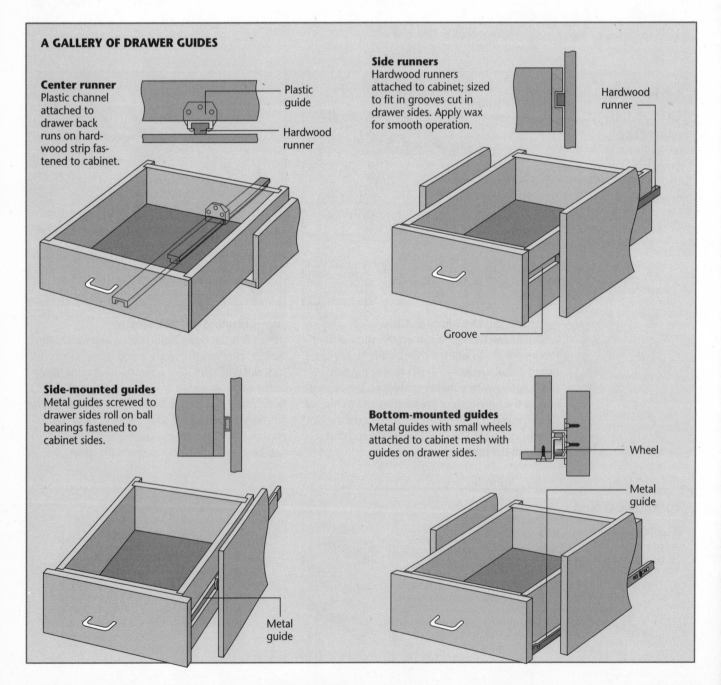

A GALLERY OF DRAWER GUIDES

Center runner
Plastic channel attached to drawer back runs on hardwood strip fastened to cabinet.

Plastic guide

Hardwood runner

Side runners
Hardwood runners attached to cabinet; sized to fit in grooves cut in drawer sides. Apply wax for smooth operation.

Hardwood runner

Groove

Side-mounted guides
Metal guides screwed to drawer sides roll on ball bearings fastened to cabinet sides.

Metal guide

Bottom-mounted guides
Metal guides with small wheels attached to cabinet mesh with guides on drawer sides.

Wheel

Metal guide

IMPROVING STORAGE AREAS

As we've shown you in the previous chapters of this book, there are many ways in which you can reorganize existing space in your basement, attic, and garage to maximize their storage potential. However, before you begin, you may want to make improvements to these areas of the house so they'll be more suitable for storage. Since these areas are not generally designed as living spaces, they may be poorly insulated and heated, as well as relatively inaccessible. Temperature and humidity swings can damage your belongings, and poor lighting and wiring can be a hazard.

In this chapter we'll give you some suggestions on the improvements that you can make, including moisture-proofing a basement, putting down an attic floor, and building a garage extension. Once you have an idea of what needs to be done, you may want to consult a professional for help.

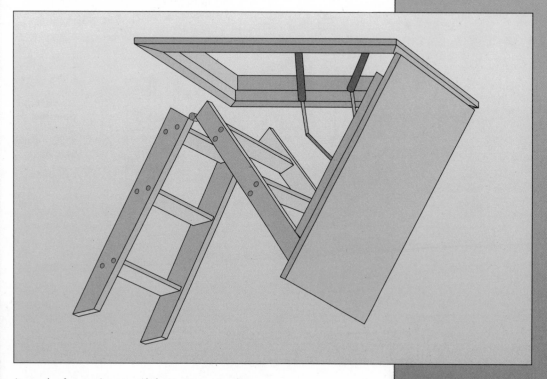

It can be frustrating—and dangerous—to clamber up a rickety ladder to stow heavy boxes in your attic. Make this space more accessible by installing a solid fold-down stairway.

BASEMENTS

Although an unfinished basement can be used for storage, you may chose to improve the area by building walls and putting down flooring. Instead of improving your entire basement, consider sectioning off an area that you can access easily and focus your efforts there. However, before installing walls and floors, you'll need to remedy any moisture problem that exists.

MOISTURE

Most basements are damp. The first step in dealing with a moisture problem is to determine whether the moisture is seeping through the wall or condensing inside the room. To test this, tape a 12-inch-square piece of plastic to the damp part of the wall, making sure the edges are sealed. Check the plastic every day for several days. If moisture droplets form on top of the plastic, the problem is condensation; if they form under the plastic, it's seepage.

If the problem is condensation, there are some simple measures you can take to control it: Wrap all water pipes with insulation, make sure the clothes dryer vents to the outside, and open the windows on cool, dry days and close them tightly on hot, humid ones. If none of these steps is effective, you may want to install a dehumidifier.

If the problem is seepage, your first step is to check for blocked roof gutters and downspouts that empty next

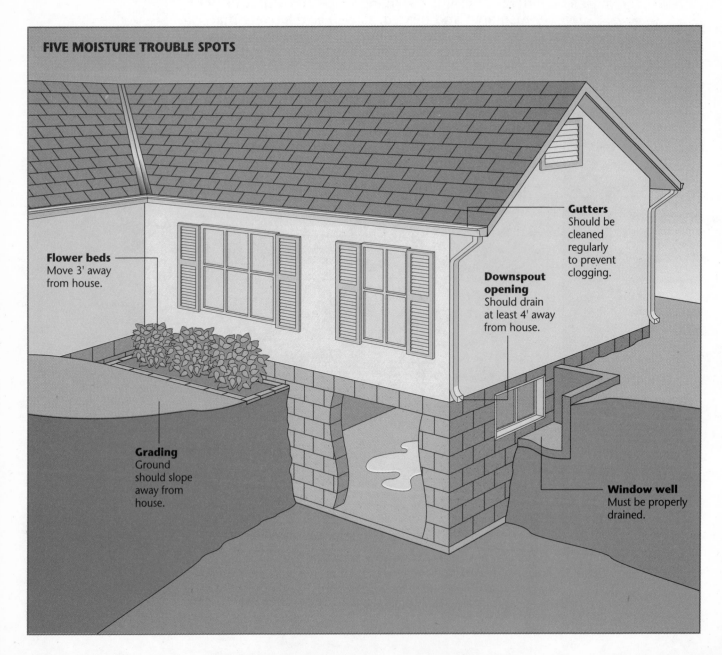

FIVE MOISTURE TROUBLE SPOTS

Gutters
Should be cleaned regularly to prevent clogging.

Downspout opening
Should drain at least 4' away from house.

Flower beds
Move 3' away from house.

Grading
Ground should slope away from house.

Window well
Must be properly drained.

to the house. Add extensions to downspouts so they drain at least 4 feet from the house. If gutters or downspouts aren't the problem, you'll need to resort to more drastic measures. Moisture-proofing paints and compounds commonly applied to basement walls and floors to prevent seepage work only temporarily.

To keep water from collecting next to the foundation, move flower beds at least 3 feet away from the house and grade the ground away from the house (at least 1 inch in 10 feet). If you can't keep water away from the house, you can apply a waterproofing membrane to the outside of the foundation walls or install French drains around the outside of the walls. Both approaches will involve major excavation. Other steps you can take include making sure window wells are well drained, installing French drains under the basement floor, or installing plastic channels with weep holes just inside the basement walls. Hook these drains up to a storm sewer or install a sump pump. All these projects are very expensive, so consult a professional before you undertake any of them. The approach to choose will depend on the source of the moisture and the degree of the problem. If your storage is hardy and the moisture problem is minor, you may decide to live with it. Turn to page 7 for a way to make storables moisture-proof.

HEATING AND COOLING

Your basement may already be heated—at least indirectly—by your house's central heating system. If not, check the system's capacity and, if possible, run new ducts to the basement space—provided you have a forced-air system. If you don't have a central heating system, consider an independent source of heat: a gas or electric heater, either portable or built-in. Check local codes for heaters that are acceptable in your area. For built-in heaters, follow the manufacturer's directions for proper ventilation. Don't leave portable heaters unattended.

You may also want to keep part of your basement cool for food or wine storage by walling off and insulating a small room. For directions, turn to page 32.

WALLS AND FLOORS

Two basic ways to put up finished basement walls are with furring strips or standard 2x4 framing. Furring strips—2x2s or 1x3s—are attached directly to masonry walls with paneling adhesive or with masonry nails (*page 73*). Walls built from 2x4s "float" in front of masonry walls—or can be positioned anywhere within the basement. They provide a better dead space for condensation control as well as extra room for thicker insulation and for wiring. They are, however, more expensive and complicated to build than furring-strip walls.

The types of insulation commonly used on basement walls include rigid polystyrene boards, fiberglass blankets, and fiberglass batts. If the insulation you choose doesn't include a vapor barrier, add a complete layer of

polyethylene over the studs and insulation; the barrier should be at least 2 mils thick. Many types of insulation must be covered with gypsum wallboard or another flame-resistant material; check local codes.

The soil itself is a good insulator. It's usually not necessary to insulate more than 2 feet below grade in many areas or below the frost line in others; check with your local building department for how far down the wall you need to insulate in your area.

Before putting down flooring, check the concrete slab for moisture by taping down a piece of plastic and checking after a few days for water droplets under the plastic. The only practical flooring choice for a basement with a serious moisture problem is ceramic tile. If the moisture problem is very minor, however, you can put down parquet with a moisture-proof adhesive, carpeting with a rubber cushion, or resilient flooring.

GETTING THE MOST OUT OF YOUR CRAWL SPACE

If you don't have a full basement, a crawl space can still provide some storage space. Your main concerns in making use of a crawl space are access, moisture, and rodents.

Your crawl space may already be accessible from the basement or the outdoors. If not, you can cut an access door through the foundation walls from outside—a very difficult project. Make sure to install a tight-fitting, locking door. You may also be able to provide access from an inconspicuous part of the house—a trap door in a kitchen pantry or a large hall closet. A ladder or steeply angled set of stairs is your best route of descent.

If your crawl space has a dirt floor, both moisture and rodents will be a problem. The simplest way to moisture-proof the area is to put down polyethylene sheeting. Hold the plastic against the foundation walls with bricks or other heavy objects. To protect your storage from rodents, use metal containers. Even with these precautions, items stored in a crawl space will be vulnerable. You may want to reserve the space for hardy items such as garden equipment.

If your crawl space is very cramped and you're pressed for storage space, you may want to investigate the cost of having a professional excavate to enlarge the area.

ATTICS

Your major enemies in an attic are swings in temperature and humidity. For very delicate storage such as books and documents, you may want to completely insulate the attic. If you don't choose to do this, you'll still have to make sure the attic is well ventilated.

You'll also want to make sure the space is accessible by installing a floor or catwalk, and a ladder or stairway. If you're converting your attic to a living area, you'll probably want to build knee walls to square off the space; for an illustration, turn to page 9.

Well-placed lights in the attic can save you a lot of anguish when you're hunting for stored items. One main attic light should be operable from a switch below; individual lights can be turned on by switches or pull chains as you move about the attic.

INSULATION

Most attics not intended as living areas are only insulated between the floor joists. However, if want to control the temperature in your attic, you'll need to insulate between the roof rafters and at the gable walls.

The most common types of insulation are blankets or batts and lightweight, rigid boards. All insulation materials are given an R-rating; the higher the number, the more effective the insulation. Check with the building department for the optimum R-rating for your area. Also check whether the type of insulation you're using needs to be covered with gypsum wallboard or another flame-resistant material.

If you're insulating the rafters and gables, a vapor barrier is necessary to prevent humid house air from condensing inside attic walls and roof materials. Blankets and batts are commonly sold with a vapor barrier of foil or kraft paper; otherwise, cover insulation with polyethylene sheeting at least 2 mils thick.

VENTILATION

Uninsulated attics need to be properly ventilated to avoid excessive buildup of heat and humidity. Natural ventilation takes advantage of thermal air movement and wind pressure; power ventilation requires an electric fan. You'll need about 1 square foot of open vent space (don't count screens or slats) per 300 square feet of floor area. Warm air can escape through vents in the gable wall, roof, and ridge line. Turbine vents set up a natural vacuum when the wind blows. The total open vent space in these spots

---

ATTIC ACCESS

If your attic is used for light or seasonal storage only—especially if it's a minimal crawl space—a trap door and folding ladder will probably be adequate. Heavier storage requires a sturdy ladder or fold-down stairs as well as a larger opening. If you'll be using the space frequently, you'll almost certainly want a fixed stairway.

Fold-down stairs, available from building suppliers or hardware stores, swing up into the ceiling to close, leaving open floor space below; they also demand little clearance above. However, they usually provide no hand support and they may lack stability. Look for a stairway with minimal bounce at the hinges. Fixed ladders are more stable, especially when fastened to a wall. A ladder's biggest drawback is steepness; it's difficult to climb up and down with full hands.

A door-size opening will admit most large storage. Width is the critical dimension, though; homeowners with limited crawl spaces can make do with a push-up hatch shorter than door size.

Look for ways to provide attic access from out-of-the-way spots. If your garage is attached, you may be able to get into the attic from the garage. You could also remove the ceiling from a large closet, install a ladder, and con-

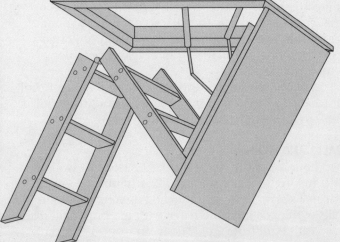

vert a crawl space above into a storage loft. Stairs or ladders adjoining a wall will be sturdier, safer, and less obtrusive than those placed further out in a room. Remember, though, that permanent stairways are often required by code to have a minimum of 6½ feet of headroom, so a permanent stair opening in the attic can't be tucked under the eaves.

must be balanced by soffit (eave) vent space that draws in cool air at the attic floor level.

Electric attic fans are inserted into a cutout in the gable wall; a fan is usually paired with an opening in the attic floor that draws air from the house below. Some fans are equipped with a thermostat. The disadvantages of electric fans are that they consume energy and make noise; some fire codes prohibit their use *(page 18)*.

Ventilating an insulated attic to avoid moisture buildup is a trickier job; you may want to consult a professional.

FLOORS

To move around your attic, you'll need to install either a catwalk or a finished floor to support your weight between joists. Attic floor joists may not be built to support the weight of human traffic or heavy storage. Before installing a catwalk or floor, inspect the joists. Check two things: spacing of the joists—joists should be 16 inches on center (or 24 inches, if the joists are

stout enough); and dimensions—joists should be at least 2x8s for heavy use, even stouter for long spans. Check with building department officials for requirements in your area. If necessary, double up the joists by adding new ones, as explained below.

A catwalk is a narrow path from the attic opening to your storage units; it's built of plywood or boards fastened to the joists. A finished floor is made of plywood. In either case 5/8-inch-thick plywood is usually adequate. However, if your joists are 24 inches on center and the floor will carry a lot of weight, use 3/4-inch plywood. Top-grade plywood isn't necessary; however, special subfloor panels with tongue-and-groove edges are stronger than standard plywood. A less expensive option than plywood is oriented-strand board.

If you can't fit standard plywood sheets (4x8 feet) through the hatch or dormer opening, cut the sheets down to a manageable size. For a catwalk, you can also use solid boards, such as 1x6s fastened side by side.

Putting in an attic floor

1 ▶ Adding new joists
If the existing joists aren't up to supporting stored items, you'll have to add new ones. Lay new joists next to existing ones, placing wood shims between the new boards and the top cap, if necessary, so the top edges of all the joists are level. Then nail the new joists to the top cap or bearing wall at each end and to the existing joists; drive a nail for every 8" to 12" of joist length, as shown at right.

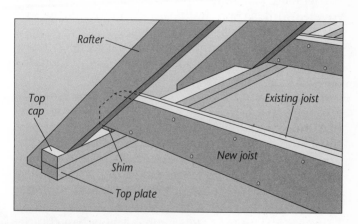

Rafter

Top cap

Existing joist

Shim

New joist

Top plate

2 ▶ Installing the flooring
Fasten nailing blocks between joists. Then lay the sheets down so their edges meet midway over a joist or nailing block, staggering panel ends in adjoining rows *(inset)*. Nail down the sheets. Check codes for the required clearance around any recessed fixtures.

If insulation extends above the joists, toenail runners atop the joists, then fasten the flooring to the runners.

This work may require some minor repairs to the ceiling.

Plywood panel

Existing joist

Nailing blocks

New joist

Plywood panel

Joists

GARAGES

If your garage (or carport) is to be used for more than parking, it may require specific improvements to ensure that it's safe, comfortable for working, weather-tight, and up to code. In addition to improving heating, plumbing, and wiring, you may want to expand the space by building an overhead loft or a garage extension. Consider the following issues:

INSULATION AND VENTILATION

You might choose to insulate your garage for either of two reasons: (1) to prevent swings in temperature that might damage storage; or (2) to make a heated garage more energy efficient. Put insulation between wall studs and rafters. Choose fiberglass batts, blankets, or rigid board insulation with a vapor barrier, or add a plastic barrier *(page 92)*. Some types of insulation need to be covered with gypsum wallboard or another flame-resistant material; check local codes.

Never leave a car running with the garage door closed. If you're using the garage for a workshop, you should install a ventilation system. A clothes dryer requires its own vent system.

HEATING

Insulation will help reduce heat loss. To provide heat, you have three options: (1) extend ducts from your central heating system to the garage (not feasible with detached garages); (2) install a separate forced-air unit in the garage (illegal in some areas); or (3) set up a built-in or portable room heater—probably your best choice. The most common types of room heaters are: electric (baseboard, portable, or quartz type) and oil or gas wall heaters (designed to fit between wall studs). Heaters placed at floor level can be a hazard due to gasoline fumes. Check local codes for acceptable types of heaters in your area as well as their required distance off the floor. In general, wall-mounted units are more efficient, but a portable unit can go where you go. CAUTION: Never leave portable heaters unattended.

LIGHTING

Try to mix natural and artificial light. To obtain more natural light, install windows and skylights, or replace a large section of a wall, or even the garage door, with translucent panels. Carports are often roofed with rippled plastic sheeting that lets in muted light. Place garage windows high to save wall space for storage.

Overhead fluorescent shop units are the most efficient for general lighting; one 4-foot double-tube unit lights up about 40 square feet. Place individual, adjustable spotlights—incandescent or fluorescent—where direct lighting is needed. Paint the garage walls and ceiling, as well as storage units, white to amplify reflected light.

WIRING

Power tools and garage lighting should be on different circuits; a tool or laundry circuit should be at least 20 amps. Install as many circuits as possible to prevent an overload. A dryer, a workshop, or an electric heater may require up to 240 volts.

Several grounded (three-prong) electrical outlets are a necessity and continuous power strips are a great convenience. Non-dedicated circuits should be protected by a ground-fault circuit interrupter—a type of outlet that instantly cuts power if it detects a current leak. You can run wires either underground or overhead from a power source to a detached garage.

PLUMBING

Laundries, photo darkrooms, garden center sinks, hose spigots, and mudrooms may require plumbing improvements. Extending plumbing to a detached garage can be a problem. Remember that outdoor pipes must be placed below the frost line (check local codes) and facilities that require plumbing must be higher than the drainage system. In climates that experience frost, plumbing systems for unheated garages or carports should be equipped with shutoff valves for the winter.

FLOORS

Concrete slab floors are standard. If you want to use your garage for work or play during the day and for car storage at night, you can protect the floor from oil leaks by laying down a layer of 10-mil polyethylene sheeting. For a more finished look, you can also paint the slab with special concrete paint. Some types of rubber flooring can also be used in a garage.

To insulate and dress up a drab slab, simply cover the floor with straw mats or colorful rugs.

MAXIMIZING SPACE

An overhead loft is an effective way to increase storage space—especially in a cramped one-car garage—and it's relatively straightforward to build. To construct the simplest type of loft, take advantage of existing ceiling joists. First inspect the joists for size and spacing, and add more joists if necessary *(page 93)*. In a one-car garage, high-quality 2x6s should be strong enough to support the weight of ordinary storage. But if you plan to walk on the surface or store heavy furniture in the loft, or if the joists must span more than 12 feet, they should be stouter than 2x6s. Joists should be spaced 16 inches on center for heavy storage. Ask your local building department about requirements in your area.

Use 5/8-inch plywood panels, or if the joists are 24 inches apart and the storage is heavy, use 3/4-inch. Install the panels as you would in an attic *(page 93)*.

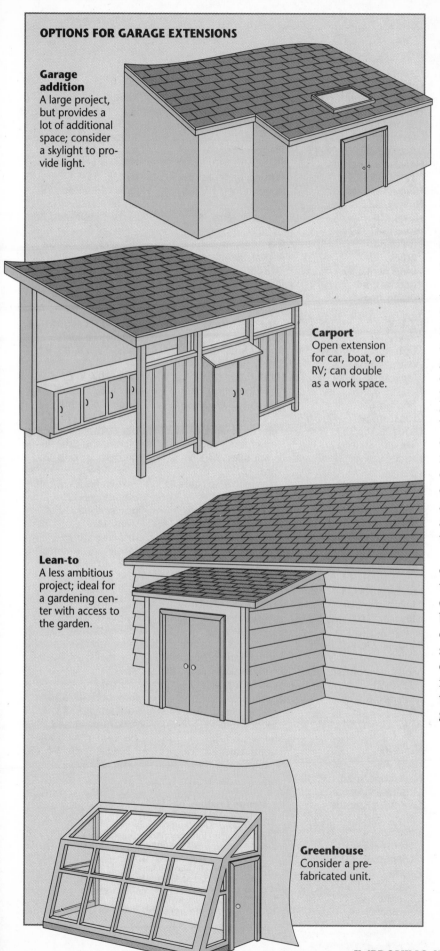

OPTIONS FOR GARAGE EXTENSIONS

Garage addition
A large project, but provides a lot of additional space; consider a skylight to provide light.

Carport
Open extension for car, boat, or RV; can double as a work space.

Lean-to
A less ambitious project; ideal for a gardening center with access to the garden.

Greenhouse
Consider a prefabricated unit.

With a peaked roof framed by trusses *(page 10)* or low collar beams, install smaller plywood platforms in the spaces between consecutive trusses (commonly 24 inches) or beams.

You've tried all the possibilities, but you just can't fit all your sports gear, garden tools, and lumber into the garage. Before you build a new structure—shed, carport, or garage— consider a simpler garage extension.

An extension represents a smaller investment in both time and money than a new structure, and takes less space. Some of your options are illustrated at left. If you're ambitious, you can also convert a one-car garage to a two-car size.

An extension borrows the garage's framework for part of its structural support. A lean-to is essentially three walls and a roof—the fourth wall is the garage. More elaborate additions entail cutting a door between the garage and an added room, or "punching out" an entire wall. In such cases, be sure to preserve adequate structural supports (headers) for the remaining garage framework. When any structural alterations are required, consult a contractor or architect for recommendations, and have your plans checked out by local building inspectors. Building codes may place limits on extension materials, height, setback from the property line, and foundation type. Also check any restrictive covenants in your deed.

Normally, an extension is built over a cast concrete slab that has been tied into the garage slab. However, a more solid foundation, extending below the frost line, may be required in colder climates. Your new extension must be weathertight: Provide a sound roof and install flashing where the extension adjoins the old garage roof or siding. Select a design, materials, and colors that match or complement both your garage and house.

INDEX

A-B-C

Adjustable shelving, 22, 59, 83, 84
Attics, 9-11
  fans, 18, 93
  floors, 10, 93
  fold-down stairways, 92
  gable walls, 10, 11
  improvements, 92-93
  sloping walls, 10
  truss framing, 10
Barbecues, 70
Bar clamps, 46
Basements, 6-8
  food cellars, 32, 33
  improvements, 90-91
  moisture problems, 6, 7, 90-91
  stairway areas, 8, 42, 65
Bicycles, 26, 57-58
Bins, 81-82
Boats, 58
Bolts, 73, 80
Books, 30
Boxes, 81-82
Bulky items, 59-66
Butt joints, 74-75
Cabinets
  file cabinets, 31
  fireproof, 22
  hidden spaces, 65
  kits, 21
  moistureproofing, 7
  rods, 82
  side doors, 65
Canned goods
  can recycling, 28, 38
  storage, 33, 34
Carpets, 60
Carports, 14, 15, 42, 95
  clearance for cars, 13
  gardening equipment, 70
  ski equipment, 55
Cases, 81
Catwalks, 93
Cedar closets, 52
Childproofing, 16
Christmas lights, 60
Closets
  for bulky items, 59
  in carports, 55, 70
  rods, 82
Clothing, 27, 52-53
  outerwear, 54
  see also Laundry areas
Clutter, 5
Commercial storage units, 20-29
Crates, 24
Crawl spaces, 6, 91
Cushions, 61

D-E-F

Dado joints, 77
Decks, 67
Design
  attics, 9-11
  basements, 6-8
  garages, 12-15
  storage areas, 5
  workshops, 43-44
Documents, 30
  file cabinets, 31
  filing boxes, 24, 30
Doors, 86-87
Dowels
  angled holes for, 79
  butt joints, 75
  for shelves, 59
Drawers, 88
Drill bits, 46
Drying racks, 54
Earthquake zones, 17, 34
Edge-glued boards, 75
Electrical circuits, 17
Emergency supplies, 34
Expansion shields, 80
Fasteners, 73
  for wallboard and masonry, 80
Fertilizer, 69
File cabinets, 31
Filing boxes, 24, 30
Fire safety, 17-18, 22
Firewood, 41-42
Flammable substances, 17-18, 22
Fold-down stairs, 92
Food, 28, 32-34
  emergency supplies, 34
  food cellars, 32, 33
  wine racks, 29, 32, 35-37
Foundations, 6
Furniture, 59, 60, 61-63
  outdoor furniture, 61

G-H-I

Game tables, 62, 63
Garages, 12-15
  clearance for cars, 13
  custom units, 66
  extensions, 95
  improvements, 94-95
  insulation, 94
  lofts, 94
  platforms, 64
Garbage containers, 38, 40
Gardening tools, 25-26, 67-70
Garden sheds, 14, 25
Garment bags, 27, 53
Gun racks, 57
Hanging shelves, 64
Hardware
  doors, 87
  fasteners, 73, 80
  storage of, 23, 48-49
Heating equipment, 18, 91, 94
Hinge mortises, 87
Hinges, 87
Hoses, 26, 67
Insects, 41, 52
Insulation
  attics, 92
  basements, 91
  garages, 94
Ironing boards, 27, 50

J-K-L-M

Joinery
  butt joints, 74-75
  dado joints, 77
  lap joints, 76-77
Joists
  finding, 79
  for storage, 7, 47, 56
Ladders, 18, 92
  see also Stairways
Ladder shelves, 8, 65, 85
Lap joints, 76-77
Larders, 33
Laundry areas, 50-51
  chutes, 51
  ironing boards, 27, 50
  supplies, 27
Lawn chairs, 61
Lazy Susans, 49
Lumber racks, 47
Magazines, 30
Masonry fasteners, 80
Mattresses, 60, 62
Modular storage units, 21, 82
Moisture problems, 6, 7, 90-91
Mortises, 87
Moths, 52
Mud rooms, 54

N-O-P-Q

Nails, 73
Newspapers, 28, 39, 40
Organizing space, 5
Overhead storage
  joists, 7, 47, 56
  pulley systems, 63
  roof spaces, 13, 14
  see also Attics
Panels
  edge-glued boards, 75
Paper items, 30-31
Peg-Board, 14, 43, 44, 78, 80
Pegs, 78, 79
Perforated hardboard, 14, 43, 44, 78, 80
Photographs, 30, 31
Pipes, 47
Plaster
  fasteners, 80
Potting benches, 68
Power tools, 17, 43, 44, 46
Pulley systems, 63

R-S

Recyclable materials, 28-29, 38-40
Rodents, 6, 91
Roof spaces
  garages, 13, 14
  see also Attics
Root cellars, 32
Router bits, 46
Safety precautions
  attics, 10
  childproofing, 16
  earthquake zones, 17, 34
  electrical circuits, 17
  emergency foods and supplies, 34
  fire, 18
  flammable substances, 17-18, 22
  guns, 57
  heating equipment, 18
  ladders and stairs, 18
  pressure-treated wood, 41, 68, 69
  storage of valuables, 14, 15, 18
  tools, 16, 17, 72
  workshops, 43
Saw blades, 46
Screws, 73
  spreading anchors and expansion shields, 80
Sewing supplies, 23
Sheds
  garden sheds, 14, 25
  woodsheds, 41
Shelves, 83-85
  adjustable, 22, 59, 83, 84
  cases, 81
  hanging shelves, 64
  ladder shelves, 8, 65, 85
  suspended, 11, 84
  see also Attics; Basements; Garages
Skis, 26, 55-56
Smoke detectors, 18
Soil, 69
Sports equipment, 26, 54-58
  bicycles, 26, 57-58
Spreading anchors, 80
Sprinkler systems, 18
Stairways,
  basements, 8, 42, 65
  fold-down, 92
  safety precautions, 18
  see also Ladders
Studs, 15, 79, 83

T-U-V-W-X-Y-Z

Tables, 62, 63, 65
Toggle bolts, 80
Tools, 23, 43-45, 72
  bar clamps, 46
  blades and bits, 46
  gardening tools, 25, 26, 67-70
  hardware, 23, 48-49
  metal racks, 25
  power tools, 17, 43-44, 46
  rust-free storage, 69
  safety precautions, 16, 17, 72
Toxic substances, 16
Truss framing, 10
Valuables, 18
  carports, 14, 15
Videocassettes, 30
Wallboard fasteners, 80
Wine racks, 29, 32, 35-37
Wood, 47
  firewood, 41-42
Workbenches, 43
Workshops, 43-49
  perforated hardboard (Peg-Board), 14, 43, 44, 78, 80

Design Credits
p. 35 *(upper)* Jean Chappell
      (lower) Ron Bogley
p. 36 *(upper)* John Hamilton, George Kelce
p. 54 *(right)* James Elliott Bryant
p. 55 *(upper)* The Hastings Group
p. 56 *(upper left)* Karlis Rekevics
p. 57 *(upper)* Glenn D. Brewer
p. 68 *(lower)* Donald Wm. MacDonald
p. 70 *(upper)* Buzz Bryan
      (lower) Armstrong and Sharfman